MW01075746

"This is not a book t
Spiritual Life of Young
a call to action; an invitation to transform how we think of and
practice ministry with young adults. Drawing on important
research from the CARA Report, this book explores how young
adults actually practice their faith and what it means for faith
communities to engage young people outside the traditional
diocesan and parish ministry models. As such, this book invites
all ministry leaders, indeed, all people of faith, to transform their
understanding of and practice of ministry with young adults."

> — Tracey Lamont, PhD, Director, Loyola Institute for
> Ministry, Loyola University New Orleans

"New lessons for new times! This book will provide you critical
insight into ministry with Hispanic young people, and crucial
aspects overlooked by previous studies. The research reaffirms the
role of authentic faith communities to accompany young people
who pray and reflect on their daily life and discern a call to service
for others. The well-informed essays will help you explore how to
foster new spiritual growth with young adults in your Catholic
community and across the country."

> — Jose Matos Auffant, National Catholic Network de
> Pastoral Juvenil Hispana (LaRED)

"This study is groundbreaking as it represents a fresh, new look at
familiar questions and expected answers. The book not only has
cultural and ethnic implications, but also offers important methods
for parishes, ecclesial movements and the church in general to
consider when doing outreach to young adults, as it reinforces the
point that affirmation of our human dignity and a welcoming
attitude are paramount for faith communities."

> — Fr. Juan J. Molina Flores, President, Mexican American
> Catholic College

"What a breath of fresh air! Amid the sobering realities and statistics we often hear about young adult Catholics, this book offers a ray of hope for what is emerging before our very eyes. Pastoral leaders and concerned Catholics will find, in *Faith and Spiritual Life of Young Adult Catholics in a Rising Hispanic Church*, hopeful news that young adults are more connected to the faith than we may have realized and that the domestic church in the home is growing in new and exciting ways. While there will certainly be challenges ahead, the insights and ideas of this book give us the confidence to face that future with our heads held high."

— Paul Jarzembowski, Associate Director for the Laity, Secretariat of Laity, Marriage, Family Life and Youth, United States Conference of Catholic Bishops

"Filled with research that is both sobering and hopeful, this book invites all of us, whether or not we primarily serve young adults or Hispanic/Latino communities, to critically reflect on the state of the church in terms of these important demographics. It is substantive in breadth and depth without losing the tactile value that supports its reader in discovering a way forward that honors the reality of our times. This research commentary is a valuable lens to which we should all hold up our ministries, asking ourselves if we are truly serving the needs of the church today."

— Nicole M. Perone, National Coordinator, ESTEEM, Founding Board Chair, National Institute for Ministry with Young Adults

Faith and Spiritual Life of Young Adult Catholics in a Rising Hispanic Church

Center for Applied Research in the Apostolate

Edited by
Thomas P. Gaunt, SJ

LITURGICAL PRESS
Collegeville, Minnesota

www.litpress.org

Cover design by John Vineyard. Photographs courtesy of Getty Images.

1   2   3   4   5   6   7   8   9

Library of Congress Cataloging-in-Publication Data

Names: Gaunt, Thomas P., editor.
Title: Faith and spiritual life of young adult Catholics in a rising
     Hispanic church : center for applied research in the apostolate /
     edited by Thomas P. Gaunt, SJ.
Description: Collegeville, Minnesota : Liturgical Press, [2022] |
     Includes bibliographical references and index. | Summary: "In a
     Church that is more culturally diverse and increasingly Hispanic,
     this book offers key insights to better understand the spirituality of
     young adult Catholics today"—Provided by publisher.
Identifiers: LCCN 2022014811 (print) | LCCN 2022014812 (ebook) |
     ISBN 9780814667958 (paperback) | ISBN 9780814667965 (epub) |
     ISBN 9780814667965 (pdf)
Subjects: LCSH: Church work with young adults—Catholic Church. |
     Hispanic American Catholics--Religion. | Christian communities. |
     Center for Applied Research in the Apostolate (U.S.)
Classification: LCC BX2347.8.Y64 F35 2022 (print) | LCC BX2347.8.Y64
     (ebook) | DDC 282/.7308968073—dc23/eng/20220602
LC record available at https://lccn.loc.gov/2022014811
LC ebook record available at https://lccn.loc.gov/2022014812

Contents

CHAPTER FIVE
**New Pastoral-Theological Directions on the Faith,
Spirituality, and Leadership Formation of Hispanic/Latinx
Youth and Young Adults in Light of CARA's Research**   73
Allan Figueroa Deck, SJ

CHAPTER SIX
**The Experiences and Perspectives of Young
Hispanics/Latines through the Pandemic**   91
Claudia Avila Cosnahan

CHAPTER SEVEN
Where Do We Go from Here?   99
Darius Villalobos

CONCLUSION
Learnings   111
Thomas P. Gaunt, SJ

APPENDIX
The CARA Research Studies Used in This Book   117
Michal J. Kramarek

References   121

Index   131

Figure

Tables

Contributors

Claudia Avila Cosnahan is the Mission & Partnerships Director for Commonweal magazine and an instructor and consultant for the Archdiocese of Los Angeles. She is a regular author of articles in Commonweal magazine.

Allan Figueroa Deck, SJ, is currently Distinguished Scholar of Pastoral Theology and Latino Studies at Loyola Marymount University. He was administrator of Our Lady of Guadalupe Church in Santa Ana, California, and first director of Hispanic Ministry for the Diocese of Orange. He was a co-founder and first president of the Academy of Hispanic Catholic Theologians of the United States (ACHTUS) and of the National Catholic Council for Hispanic Ministry (NCCHM). In 2008, he served as first director of the Secretariat of Cultural Diversity in the Church of the United States Conference of Catholic Bishops (USCCB) in Washington, DC. Fr. Deck has authored or edited nine books and published more than fifty articles and chapters in books on pastoral theology, Hispanic/Latino ministry, Catholic Social Teaching, spirituality, and faith and culture. His most recent books are *Francis, Bishop of Rome* (2016) and *365 Días con los Santos* (2021).

Thomas P. Gaunt, SJ, is a Jesuit priest and executive director of CARA. His PhD is in City and Regional Planning from the University of North Carolina at Chapel Hill. He has served in Jesuit governance as the socius/executive secretary of the Jesuit Conference USA and was the formation and studies director of the Maryland and New York Jesuit Provinces. After ordination, he spent ten years as a pastor and as director of planning and research in the Diocese of Charlotte. He has co-authored or edited three books at CARA, including *Catholic Parishes in the 21st Century*, *Pathways to Religious Life*, and *Catholic Bishops in the United States: Church Leadership in the Third Millennium*.

Mark M. Gray is the Director of CARA Catholic Polls (CCP) and a Senior Research Associate at CARA. He has a PhD in Political Science and an MA in Social Sciences from the University of California, Irvine. Methodologically, Mark specializes in survey research, trend analysis, and cross-sectional time-series studies. Some of his recent work at CARA has included national surveys of adult Catholics, surveys for Catholic schools, diocesan-level trend analyses, program evaluations, and Catholic media studies. Academically, his research focuses on political culture, political participation, religion and politics, mass media, and popular culture. His research has appeared in *Comparative Political Studies*, *International Organization*, *Review of Religious Research*, *PS: Political Science & Politics*, *Journal for the Scientific Study of Religion*, *Presidential Studies Quarterly*, *European Review*, and *Catholic Education: A Journal of Inquiry and Practice*.

Michal J. Kramarek is a CARA Research Associate and the editor of the *Catholic Ministry Formation Directory*. He holds a PhD in Philanthropic Studies from Indiana University in Indianapolis, a Certificate in Nonprofit Studies from Johns Hopkins University, and an MA in Corporate Finance and Accounting from a school in Poland. Michal works on personnel projections, employee compensation studies, program evaluations, and membership surveys. He has authored a half-dozen book chapters as well as dozens of reports and white papers serving the needs of the Catholic Church.

Hosffman Ospino is an Associate Professor of Theology and Religious Education at Boston College School of Theology and Ministry where he is also Chair of the Department of Religious Education and Pastoral Ministry. He received a PhD in Theology and Education from Boston College. Dr. Ospino's research concentrates on the dialogue between theology and culture and the impact of this interchange upon Catholic theological education, catechesis, and ministry. He has served as the principal investigator for several national studies on Hispanic Catholics. He has authored or edited 15 books and more than 150 essays, academic and general. He is the President of the Academy of Catholic Hispanic Theologians of the United States (ACHTUS) and serves on the boards of several academic and ministerial organizations.

Darius Villalobos serves as the Director of Diversity and Inclusion for the National Federation for Catholic Youth Ministry (NFCYM). He previously served in the Archdiocese of Chicago in a variety of ministry roles, including youth ministry, young adult ministry, evangelization, and catechesis. He currently serves on the National Advisory Team for Young Adult Ministry of the United States Conference of Catholic Bishops (USCCB) and as a founding board member of the National Institute for Ministry with Young Adults. He was born and raised in Chicago and is a graduate of DePaul University, where he received his bachelor's degree in English and Catholic Studies. Darius is a Bernardin Scholar at the Catholic Theological Union in Chicago in the Master of Arts in Intercultural Ministry program. He has served as a parish RCIA director, liturgical music minister, retreat director, catechist, and youth minister.

Patricia Wittberg, SC, is a Sister of Charity of Cincinnati, Ohio. She holds a PhD in sociology from the University of Chicago and is currently a research associate with CARA. She is the author of numerous books and articles on Catholicism and Catholic religious life, including her most recent book, *Migration for Mission: International Catholic Sisters in the United States.*

Acknowledgments

The CARA researchers are grateful for the support of generous benefactors to the work of CARA that enabled this research on the faith engagement and spiritual life of young adult Catholics in the United States. Our research and writing was aided by the assistance of Ignacio Garrido Cruz of Cordoba, Spain, with interviews, Mary Gautier of Mobile, Alabama, with editing, and Connie Neuman of Bethesda, Maryland, with indexing. We are also grateful for the coverage of our research given by *America* magazine in the fall of 2021.

Categories to name people that the US Census Office identifies as US Hispanic and those of Latin American and Caribbean heritage and culture are often debated. In this book, we honor the terms each author has chosen to refer to this diverse population. Doing so highlights particular sensibilities in the way authors articulate self-understandings, the complexity of this sociocultural experience, and some generational shifts.

Introduction

Mark M. Gray

In recent years, social scientists and pollsters have noted a significant shift toward secularization among young adults in the United States. For example, a 2016 review of survey data by the Public Religion Research Institute (PRRI) concluded, "Today, nearly four in ten (39%) young adults (ages 18-29) are religiously unaffiliated—three times the unaffiliated rate (13%) among seniors (ages 65 and older). While previous generations were also more likely to be religiously unaffiliated in their twenties, young adults today are nearly four times as likely as young adults a generation ago to identify as religiously unaffiliated."[1] The Pew Research Center drew similar conclusions in 2015, noting, "The Christian share of the U.S. population is declining, while the number of U.S. adults who do not identify with any organized religion is growing. . . . While the drop in Christian affiliation is particularly pronounced among young adults, it is occurring among Americans of all ages."[2]

The General Social Survey (GSS) indicates young Catholics have been increasingly leaving the faith in which they were

---

[1] Robert Jones et al., *Exodus: Why Americans Are Leaving Religion—and Why They're Unlikely to Come Back* (Washington, DC: Public Religion Research Institute, 2016), 3.

[2] See Pew Research Center, "America's Changing Religious Landscape: Demographic Study," May 12, 2015, https://www.pewforum.org/wp-content/uploads/sites/7/2015/05/RLS-08-26-full-report.pdf.

raised. In 1973, 84 percent of those raised Catholic in the United States remained Catholics as adults, with only 6 percent disaffiliating and reporting no religious affiliation. This trend remained steady until the early 1990s. Catholic affiliation rates then began to fall, and the share not identifying with any religion began to rise. In 2018, only 64 percent of those raised Catholic remained Catholic as adults, and 19 percent had no religious affiliation.[3] A 2017 study, *Going, Going, Gone,* found that the median age at which young Catholics are disaffiliating is 13.[4]

Among the Catholics who remain in the faith into young adulthood, the statistics also point to lower levels of engagement, comparatively speaking. For example, Pew's 2015 report indicates younger Millennial Catholics (born 1990-1996) attend religious services less often than any other Christian group.[5] They estimate that 26 percent of younger Millennial Catholics attend at least once a week, compared to 58 percent of Evangelical Protestants, 48 percent of Historically Black Protestants, and 32 percent of mainline Protestants of the same generation.

Looking beyond these religious retention rates and frequencies of weekly Mass attendance, this book explores something new: how young adult Catholics are practicing their faith in ways that may not be captured in the traditional survey research questions used for decades by sociologists of religion. Specifically, it looks at participation of young adult Catholics in Small Christian Communities. These are, relatively speaking, an understudied phenomenon. In 2000, Bernard Lee conducted one of the few existing studies of these groups; describing them, he wrote, "Christians are gathering on their

---

[3] Tom Smith et al., *General Social Surveys, 1972–2018* (Chicago: National Opinion Research Center [NORC], 2019).

[4] Robert J. McCarty and John M. Vitek, *Going, Going, Gone: The Dynamics of Disaffiliation in Young Catholics* (Winona, MN: St. Mary's Press, 2017), 74.

[5] Pew Research Center, "America's Changing Religious Landscape."

own initiative to form communities—usually small ones that are often supported by priests and religious sisters and brothers. But the membership and leadership are largely lay."[6]

These emerging lay communities are often informal and outside of the traditional parish setting. They may involve domestic settings and include prayer, Bible study, and other forms of worship and practice. Thus, these communities' activities are not often captured by surveys about religion that focus on attendance at religious services, parish registration, parish giving, or the reception of sacraments. To what extent are young adult Catholics participating in these communities? Do they participate in them as well as in their parishes, or has this become a new way of practicing the faith without engaging in traditional parish life? How did these communities fare during the COVID-19 pandemic when many Catholics could not engage in parish life in ways they have in the past?

This volume is based on two recent national surveys from the Center for Applied Research in the Apostolate (CARA): one of young adult Catholics and the other of members of Small Christian Communities. The first two chapters broadly explore the results of these surveys. The chapters that follow provide commentary on these results and explore important differences by ethnicity, within families and households, across generations, and specifically among Hispanic Catholics—the fastest-growing segment of the Catholic Church in the United States. What these results mean for the Catholic Church and its approach to young adults is also explored.

What unfolds in this volume is an examination of the ways in which many young adult Catholics are now active in their faith but not necessarily in the traditional context. We also examine why they are making these choices. We find some are disillusioned with their parish and its leadership. Some have

---

[6] Bernard Lee, *The Catholic Experience of Small Christian Communities* (New York: Paulist Press, 2000), 5.

concerns about specific Church teachings. Others just say they prefer to practice their faith outside of traditional parish life. These results provide a more complete portrait of how young adult Catholics are practicing their faith—a portrait that has been largely missing in existing research about young adults and religion and that offers a glimpse of a much more active faith life than what has been noted in research in recent years.

CHAPTER ONE

Faith Group Activity among Catholic Young Adults

Mark M. Gray

Introduction

This first chapter provides a national overview of how young adult Catholics in the United States live out their faith, in parishes and, more notably, at home and in their communities. Results presented here are from a national survey including 2,214 young adults between the ages of eighteen and thirty-five during the summer of 2020. The margin of sampling error for the survey is ±3.6 percentage points. A fuller explanation of the methodology is available in the Appendix.

The Faith Life of Young Adult Catholics

Most young adult Catholics report that they have had some form of religious education and/or formation in their youth. Three in four young adult Catholics have participated in parish-based religious education and/or a parish youth group as a minor. Eight in ten entered the faith as an infant or a child. Eighty-two percent have received their First Communion, and 73 percent have been confirmed. A third have attended a Catholic school at some point between kindergarten and twelfth grade.

The young adult Catholic respondents surveyed were presented with a list of Church-related programs and groups and asked if they had ever participated in any of these. This list included some groups that are Small Christian Communities and lay movements. Overall, 37 percent of respondents indicated that they have done so at some point. They were most likely to report having participated in a parish or diocesan young adult group (15%), a religious institute volunteer group (9%), Knights of Columbus (6%), pro-life events or groups (5%), or in a St. Vincent de Paul Society group (4%). Three percent or fewer have participated in a named Small Christian Community (SCC). While these percentages may be small, they represent sizable populations. Even 1 percent of the young adult Catholic population represents approximately 200,000 individuals.

Some of the "other" groups named by 3 percent of respondents included altar server, choir, mission trips, RCIA (Rite of Christian Initiation of Adults), names of parishes or schools, Vacation Bible School, and youth group. Others indicated that they participate in Bible study, Catholic Daughters of the Americas, Catholic Women of the Chapel, Conquistando las Naciones para Cristo, Emaus, Fellowship of Christian Athletes, FOCUS (Fellowship of Catholic University Students), Frassati Society of Young Adult Catholics, Theology on Tap, Young Life, or Youth for Christ.

Respondents were asked if they participate in any Catholic group or community of people with whom they regularly meet, outside of Mass, to practice their faith, provide service or assistance to others, or evangelize and spread their faith to others. Overall, 46 percent of Catholic young adults reported that they were active in a group that does at least one of these three things. They were most likely to indicate they were active in groups that practice the faith (e.g., Bible study, prayer, devotions, and/or faith sharing).

Finally, we asked respondents about the ways they practiced their Catholic faith with others outside of the parish or attend-

Table 1.1

Have you ever participated in any of the following Church-related programs, groups, or activities as an adult?

	Percentage "Yes"
Parish or diocesan young adult group	15%
Religious institute volunteer (e.g., Mercy Volunteer Corps)	9%
Knights of Columbus	6%
Pro-life events/groups	5%
St. Vincent de Paul Society	4%
Jóvenes Para Cristo	3%
Legion of Mary	2%
Charismatic Renewal	2%
Cursillo	2%
Amor en Acción	1%
Movimiento Familiar Cristiano	1%
Juan XXIII	1%
Neocatechumenal Way	1%
Other	3%

Source: Data from *Faith and Spiritual Life of Catholics in the United States* (Washington, DC: Center for Applied Research in the Apostolate, 2021).

ing Mass prior to the pandemic as an open-ended question where respondents answered in their own words. These were coded and categorized. Ten percent of responses to this question describe an activity consistent with participation in Small Christian Communities, lay movements, and other forms of practicing the faith with others (non-family) outside of the parish.

Once the responses to all three of these questions are combined, we can discern that a majority of young adult Catholics, 60 percent, indicate in some way that they are practicing their faith outside of attending Mass at their parish. Overall, 13 percent of young adult Catholics attended Mass weekly or more often prior to the pandemic. Twenty-one percent attended less than weekly but at least once a month. Two-thirds of respondents attended Mass a few times a year or less often.

Using frequency of Mass attendance (prior to the pandemic) and respondent reports of faith group participation, we can separate the sample into four groups, as shown in Table 1.2. About a quarter of young adult Catholics is active in parish life as well as in faith groups outside of Mass attendance and their parish. The smallest group includes those who attend Mass at least once a month and do not participate in any other faith group (7%). A third attends Mass infrequently and does not participate in a faith group. Finally, 34 percent of Catholic young adults indicate they are infrequent Mass attenders but do participate in a faith group outside of Mass attendance at their parish.

Anecdotally, infrequent attenders—especially young people—are often assumed to be generally inactive in their faith. Yet, it appears that one in three Catholic young adults who are infrequent attenders are still active in their faith—just outside of the traditional parish context.

Respondents who attend Mass less than weekly were presented with a list of reasons why they might have missed Mass prior to the pandemic. Among young adult Catholics who do attend Mass less than weekly, the two reasons that most frequently apply to all of these respondents, regardless of their participation in a faith group, is a busy schedule or a lack of time and a belief that missing Mass is not a sin.

Among those young adult Catholics who attend Mass a few times a year or less often (i.e., less than monthly) and who also participate in a faith group, the next most important reason for missing Mass is a preference to practice their faith outside of the parish (49%). Among those who participate in faith groups and attend Mass at least monthly, family responsibili-

Table 1.2

Mass attendance and faith group participation.

	Participates in faith group(s) outside of Mass and parish	Does not participate in faith group(s)
Attends Mass at least monthly or more often	26%	7%
Attends Mass a few times a year or less often	34%	33%

Source: Data from *Faith and Spiritual Life of Catholics in the United States* (Washington, DC: Center for Applied Research in the Apostolate, 2021).

ties are also a frequently cited reason for missing Mass (57%). This is also the case for monthly attendees who do not participate in any faith groups (46%). For those who attend Mass infrequently and who do not participate in any faith group, another commonly cited reason is viewing oneself as "not a very religious person" (53%).

Despite anecdotes that may be frequently noted, feeling alienated with the Church is seldom cited by young adult Catholics as a reason they miss Mass. Feeling that Mass does not meet their spiritual needs is also relatively infrequently cited as a reason for this.

All respondents were asked about things that might make them less likely to be active in parish life. Among those who attend Mass less than monthly but who participate in faith groups, the things most likely to make young adults less active in their parish were the Church's teachings on homosexuality (42% saying this makes them "somewhat" or "very" less likely to be active), allegations of clergy sexually abusing minors (41%), feeling older generations have too much influence in

Table 1.3

How well did each of the following explain, if at all, why you missed Mass?

Percentage of those who attend Mass less than weekly responding "Somewhat" or "Very Much" combined by frequency of Mass attendance and faith group participation

	Participates in a Faith Group		Does Not Participate in a Faith Group	
	<Monthly Mass Attender	Monthly+ Mass Attender	<Monthly Mass Attender	Monthly+ Mass Attender
Busy schedule or lack of time	56%	64%	55%	57%
I don't believe missing Mass is a sin	55%	47%	61%	41%
I prefer to practice my faith outside of the parish	49%	36%	43%	16%
Family responsibilities	44%	57%	37%	46%
I am not a very religious person	43%	25%	53%	28%
Inconvenient Mass schedule	34%	43%	30%	39%
Masses don't meet my spiritual needs	32%	24%	35%	19%
I find Mass too boring	28%	27%	40%	14%
Conflict with work	27%	38%	23%	29%
I feel alienated from the Church	24%	22%	24%	8%
Out of town travel	23%	38%	14%	31%
Health problems or a disability	17%	32%	8%	23%
Unable to find transportation	14%	26%	8%	20%
I am divorced or married outside of the Church	12%	16%	6%	8%

Source: Data from *Faith and Spiritual Life of Catholics in the United States* (Washington, DC: Center for Applied Research in the Apostolate, 2021).

Table 1.4

How much, if at all, have the following ever made you less likely to be active in parish life?

Percentage of responding "Somewhat" or "Very" combined by frequency of Mass attendance and faith group participation

	Participates in a Faith Group		Does Not Participate in a Faith Group	
	<Monthly Mass Attender	Monthly+ Mass Attender	<Monthly Mass Attender	Monthly+ Mass Attender
The Church's teachings on homosexuality	42%	40%	47%	32%
Allegations of Catholic clergy sexually abusing minors	41%	44%	46%	39%
Feeling that older generations have too much influence in the parish	39%	40%	32%	20%
The roles available to women in the Church	37%	36%	28%	22%
The Church's teachings on the use of birth control	36%	35%	33%	28%
Feeling like the Church is not open to dialogue with other religious faiths	34%	36%	32%	17%
My perception of the Church's participation in politics and elections	33%	35%	29%	16%
Being asked for donations	31%	33%	28%	16%
The Church's teachings on divorce and remarriage	31%	34%	33%	22%
The parish is not welcoming to different ethnic or cultural Catholic groups	28%	32%	20%	10%
The parish is not welcoming to young adults	26%	29%	21%	17%
The parish is not welcoming to a family member or friend	24%	28%	15%	12%
Feeling like the parish is not sufficiently adhering to the traditions of the Church	22%	30%	15%	15%

Source: Data from *Faith and Spiritual Life of Catholics in the United States* (Washington, DC: Center for Applied Research in the Apostolate, 2021).

the parish (39%), and the roles available to women in the Church (37%). Other respondents with varying frequencies of Mass attendance and involvement with faith groups have a similar ranking of the issues that prevent them from being more active in their parish.

The reasons that are among the least likely to be keeping young adults who attend Mass less than monthly but who are active in a faith group from being active in their parish are feeling like the parish is not adhering to the traditions of the Church (22%), the parish not being welcoming to a family member or friend (24%), the parish not welcoming young adults (26%), and the parish not welcoming different ethnic or cultural groups (28%). Respondents who are not active in faith groups are even less likely to say these things make them less likely to be active in parish life.

Thus, young adults are not as likely to report a feeling that they or friends and family feel unwelcome at their parish and are more likely to bring up issues related to Church teachings or scandal as keeping them away.

Generally speaking, young adult Catholics who participate in faith groups are more likely than those who do not participate in these to have experienced the sacraments of initiation, to have been involved in Catholic youth groups as a child, and to have attended Catholic schools and/or been involved in parish-based religious education. Thus, some of the motivation for their desire to be active in groups related to their faith may be an extension of habits and norms they developed in their childhood.

There are few demographic differences between respondents in their self-reporting of being active in a faith group. Women are similarly likely to be active as men (59% compared to 61%). Non-Hispanic White respondents are only slightly less likely than Hispanic respondents to be active in a group (56% compared to 61%). One outlier are young adult Black Catholics who are especially likely to be active in a faith group

(88%).[1] Respondents with a high school education only are slightly more likely than those with a college degree to be active in a group (64% compared to 57%). Group activity is slightly higher in the West than in the Midwest (63% compared to 57%).

Faith group participants are different than non-participants in a number of other ways. A majority of faith group participants, 55 percent, agree that they think of themselves as a practicing Catholic compared to 27 percent of non-participants. At the same time, faith group participants are more likely than non-participants to agree that there have been times recently when they have struggled with their faith (50% compared to 39%). Even with these struggles, faith group participants are more likely than non-participants to agree that they could never imagine themselves leaving the Catholic Church (47% compared to 28%). Given that many faith groups have a service component, faith group participants are also more likely than non-participants to agree that helping the poor and needy is a moral obligation for Catholics (63% compared to 50%).

Respondents who are active in faith groups were asked to evaluate a list of possible motivations for their participation. They were most likely to indicate that the following were "somewhat" or "very much" a motivation for them: a desire to learn from new experiences (74%), to nourish their spiritual life (70%), to reduce negative feelings (69%), and to act or express important convictions concerning serving others (69%).

The survey provides some evidence that those involved in faith groups may be more likely than those who are not faith group participants to be socially active with non-family

---

[1] Of note, there were 109 Black respondents in the survey (unweighted). The margin of error for this subgroup is nearly 10 percentage points. Even with this possible variation, it appears Black Catholic young adults are indeed among the most likely to participate in faith groups; however, one cannot say with precision at what level this occurs.

members. Nearly half of those involved in a faith group (48%) say that, prior to the pandemic, they would spend a social evening with someone in their neighborhood at least once a month, compared to about a third of those (32%) who are not involved in a faith group. Faith group participants are also slightly more likely than others to spend a social evening with someone who lives outside their neighborhood (60% compared to 50%). There is no difference between these two groups in terms of spending a social evening with a relative at least once a month (73% of faith group participants compared to 69% of non-participants).

Faith group participants are also more likely than those who are not involved with one of these groups to invite a non-family member to their home at least once a month for a meal (50% compared to 40%) or for faith sharing or prayer (27% compared to 4%). Faith group participants are also more likely than non-participants to go to a non-family member's home at least once a month for a meal (49% compared to 39%) or for faith sharing or prayer (25% compared to 3%).

Profiles of Faith Group Activity

The previous section explored who is participating in faith groups and what they told us about why they do so. This section details what respondents told us about their faith groups and what they do in them.

When presented with a list of different types of faith-related groups and asked if their group fits these, the most common group selected was a Bible study community (15%). Twelve percent said their group was a Hispanic/Latino community. Nine percent said their group was a choir, and 8 percent said it was a youth group. Seven percent said their faith group was part of a parish community, and 6 percent said it was a Rosary circle. Less often, respondents described their group as a college student community (5%), charismatic community (5%),

Table 1.5

At a typical community meeting, did you engage in any of the following?

Percentage of Catholics, ages 18-35, who participate in Catholic group or community

	Percentage "Yes"
Prayer	65%
Socializing	36%
Reading and discussing scripture	30%
Faith sharing	29%
Group silence	23%
Discussing spirituality	19%
Raising money or collecting donations	18%
Recreational group activities	15%
Directly serving others	15%
Eucharist	14%
Sharing religious visions	12%
Discussion on political or social issues	10%
Evangelization	7%
Advocacy	7%
Administrative/business matters	6%
Promotion of ecumenical/interfaith dialogue	5%
Other activities	3%

Source: Data from *Faith and Spiritual Life of Catholics in the United States* (Washington, DC: Center for Applied Research in the Apostolate, 2021).

associate community of a religious order (4%), retreat (4%), or Eucharistic-centered community (3%).

Prior to the pandemic, 55 percent of those participating in a faith group were active in their group at least once a month. About one in ten were active more than once a week, one in ten were only active quarterly, and 30 percent were active seasonally. The most common location of meeting for the group was within a parish (41%). However, more often than not, the activity is done somewhere else, such as a school, college, or university (21%), a public space (21%), in members' homes (20%), a community-owned space (17%), or a convent or monastery (8%). Thirteen percent note meeting online and 5 percent in some other space that was not listed.

Faith group participants were asked to describe what they did at group meetings prior to the pandemic. By far, the most common activity was prayer (65%). This was followed by socializing (36%), reading and discussing scripture (30%), faith sharing (29%), group silence (23%), and discussing spirituality (19%). Less often, group activities included raising money or collecting donations (18%), recreational group activities (15%), directly serving others (15%), or the Eucharist (14%). Among the types of activities done least often were evangelization (7%) and advocacy (7%). This may represent a more inward focus of these groups other than their participation in providing service to others.

Respondents were also asked to whom their group provides service. Young adults are the most common group served by the respondents' faith group (67% of communities). These groups also commonly serve families, couples, and single parents (56%), seniors (55%), minors (54%), the homeless, hungry, and poor (52%), and the sick and disabled (40%). A third say they serve those people seeking to deepen their faith, and 30 percent serve parishioners. Among those groups less likely to be served are victims of disasters (27%), people of a particular nationality or race/ethnicity (21%), the unborn (18%), and prisoners (17%).

All respondents were asked generally about volunteering and service. Faith group participants are significantly more likely than non-participants to be involved in volunteering and service projects. Faith group participants are also more likely than non-participants to work with others at least a few times a year on a community service project (52% compared to 20%), a service project outside of their community (44% compared to 12%), volunteering at a school (49% compared to 18%), helping neighbors (70% compared to 47%), volunteering at a food bank (41% compared to 11%), or visiting the sick or elderly (44% compared to 14%). When asked how important their Catholic faith is in motivating them to provide this service and volunteering, 55 percent of faith group participants agreed that their Catholic faith motivated them "somewhat" or "very much," compared to 25 percent of non-participants.

Faith During the Pandemic

As the pandemic began in early 2020, Catholic young adults were just beginning the Lenten period of the Church calendar, which tends to be among the most active for practicing faith during the year. Fifty-three percent of young adults said they abstained from meat on Fridays during Lent. Thirty-nine percent gave up something for Lent, other than meat on Fridays. Thirty-five percent received ashes on Ash Wednesday. This is likely fewer than would have done this in more typical years, as news of American COVID-19 infections and lockdowns restricting people from participating in group activities began before that Wednesday. Members of faith groups were among the most likely young adult Catholics to participate in all of these Lenten observations in 2020. Fifty-nine percent of faith group members abstained from meat on Fridays, 46 percent gave something up for Lent, and 45 percent received ashes.

As American communities went into lockdown, most young adult Catholics active in faith groups prayed as frequently as they did before the pandemic. However, 35 percent said that they began to pray more, and 13 percent indicated less frequent prayer. Overall, 18 percent of young adult Catholics indicated that they had been contacted by their parish during the pandemic. However, those active in faith groups were much more likely than those who were not to report their parish reaching out to them (26% compared to 6%). Some reported phone calls and emails, but many indicated being messaged on social media. Often, the parish was checking in on them. They also often reported that their parish offered them financial assistance, food, and religious resources.

Fifty-nine percent of faith group members said they watched Masses on television or online at least "a little" during the pandemic (19% "somewhat" often and 16% "very often"). Just more than three in ten faith group members video chatted with other parishioners or members of their faith group during lockdowns.

Respondents were asked about their expectations after the pandemic ends. Most members of faith groups, 50 percent, said they intend on attending Mass with the same frequency after the pandemic as they did before it began. Fourteen percent plan to attend more frequently, and 36 percent say they intend to go to Mass less often. There is even more discomfort in returning to the norms of participating in faith groups. Forty-three percent of group members say they plan to participate in their faith group just as they did before. Fourteen percent plan to participate more frequently, and 43 percent say they intend to be less active. Thus, at least at the time of the survey, unease about the pandemic led many young adult Catholics to question the way they will participate in their faith in the post-pandemic future.

Overall, one in five young adult Catholics say their faith has been strengthened during the pandemic. Most, 71 percent, say their faith has been unchanged. Just 8 percent indicate that their faith has weakened. Members of faith groups are among the most likely to say their faith was strengthened (27%), and just 7 percent say the pandemic weakened their faith. Thus, while some are considering being less active in their faith post-pandemic, this is unlikely to be because their underlying religious faith has changed.

Conclusion

Young adult Catholics are much more likely to be involved in faith groups outside of attending Mass or their parish life than what is acknowledged publicly. This participation appears to be grounded in a desire to live out their faith in daily life and the fact that these participants are generally more socially active than non-participants. It will likely surprise many that a significant segment of young adult Catholics are interested in and already regularly participating in Bible study and social prayer—often outside of the parish context.

In addition to often having a preference to participate in their faith outside of the parish context, faith group participants also appear to be concerned about being more involved with their parish because of the Church's teachings on homosexuality, allegations of clergy sexually abusing minors, feeling that older generations have too much influence in the parish, and the roles available to women in the Church.

It is still unclear how young adult Catholics will change their participation in these groups or parish life after the COVID-19 pandemic ends. The survey that asked respondents about their intentions took place in the context of the pandemic before vaccines were available. Yet there appears to be a lot of hesitancy about the future among young adult Catholics. At the same time, it would seem unlikely that the more socially active faith group participants would not seek out the opportunity to live their faith in and to provide service to their communities as they did prior to the pandemic.

A final note on how faith group membership is conceptualized is important for the chapters that follow. This initial chapter has looked at membership in the broadest terms possible by combining all respondents who indicated participation by membership in a named group, indicated participation in a group with some "other" purpose, and/or noted faith group participation in response to an open-ended question about how they practice their faith. Some of the analysis that follows may focus in on one type of indication of participation. This is especially important in evaluating participation in Small Christian Communities (SCC) and Movements. This is best measured by respondents indicating their membership in a specific named and established group.

It is also important to note that this chapter has focused on all Catholic young adults. In the chapters that follow, there is more focus on Hispanic young adult Catholics, a group that has increased in number among the eighteen- to thirty-five-year-old cohort of Catholics in the last two decades. About three in ten young adult Catholics self-identified as Hispanic in the 2000 General Social Survey (GSS). Just before 2020, 44 percent of Catholic young adults self-identified as Hispanic. This trend is expected to continue in the years ahead. To some extent, how young adult Hispanic Catholics are engaging in their faith today could be a window into how most young adult Catholics will do so in the future.

CHAPTER TWO

Young Catholics in Small Christian Communities: Who They Are and Why They Get Involved

Michal J. Kramarek

[Small Christian Communities] are a sign of vitality within the Church, an instrument of formation and evangelization, and a solid starting point for a new society based on a "civilization of love."

—Pope St. John Paul II[1]

I love belonging to this community because I am surrounded with students/friends my age that are also committed to their faith, as well as many strong leaders like staff and religious who help guide, lead, and form my growth.

—Small Christian Community member

Introduction

The previous chapter provided a "big picture" description of young adult Catholics in America. This next chapter focuses on those young adult Catholics who are involved in Small Christian Communities. Young adults are defined as people

---

[1] John Paul II, Encyclical *Redemptoris Missio: On the Permanent Validity of the Church's Missionary Mandate* (Rome: December 7, 1990), 51.

between eighteen and thirty-five years old who self-identify as Catholic. Involvement in a Small Christian Community is defined as regular participation (at least once a quarter or seasonally) pre-pandemic. Small Christian Communities[2] are defined as Catholic groups or communities of people meeting to practice their faith (e.g., Bible study, prayer, devotions, faith sharing), to provide service or assistance to others, and/or to evangelize and spread their faith to others. (Note that this definition, also used in Chapter 3, is different from the definitions used in Chapter 1).[3] The chart below shows examples of different groups in which those young adult Catholics have participated.[4]

---

[2] Despite being called Small Christian Communities, some of these groups may have many members. In CARA's study, it was up to the study participants to define what "small" means. Some groups may have a large number of members but still be able to offer a small community experience. Small Christian Communities do not include communities of men and women religious.

[3] In the literature, Small Christian Communities "are called faith communities, faith groups, faith sharing groups, base communities, basic Christian communities, basic ecclesial communities, house churches, small church communities, small Christian communities, intentional Eucharistic communities, charismatic communities, and so forth. Reverend Joseph Healey, a Maryknoll missionary in Africa, has collected over a thousand ways of labeling these groups." See Bernard Lee, *The Catholic Experience of Small Christian Communities* (New York: Paulist Press, 2000).

[4] Other examples identified in the study include: Asociacion de Hermanas Latinas Misioneras en America; Asociacion Jovenes Para Cristo; Asociacion Nacional de Diaconos Hispanos; Asociacion Nacional de Sacerdotes Hispanos; Call to Action; Catholic Association of Latino Leaders; Catholic Charismatic Renewal; El Comité Nacional de Servicio Hispano (CNSH) de la Renovación Carismática Católica (RCC); Federacion de Institutos Pastorales (FIP); Focolare Movement; FOCUS Missionaries; Institute of Faith and Life/ Instituto Fe y Vida; Instituto Nacional Hispano de Liturgia; Intentional Eucharistic Communities; Knights of Columbus College Councils; Lay Dominicans; Secular Lay Franciscans; Marianist Lay Network of North America; Instituto Nacional Hispano de Liturgia; National Alliance for Parish Restructuring into Communities; National Association of the Holy Name Society; National Catholic Association of Diocesan Directors for Hispanic Ministry; National Catholic Council for Hispanic Ministry; National Catholic Network

Figure 2.1

Have you ever participated in any of the following Church-related programs, groups, or activities as an adult?

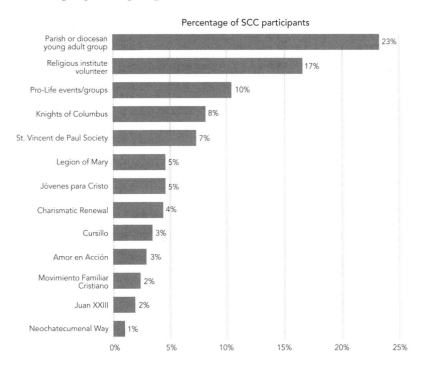

Percentage of SCC participants

Source: Data from *Faith and Spiritual Life of Catholics in the United States* (Washington, DC: Center for Applied Research in the Apostolate, 2021).

Young adult Catholics involved in Small Christian Communities are an important group for the Church to understand. For instance, they are a relatively large group that is estimated to include 9.3 million people—45 percent of US Catholic young adults or 10 percent of all US young adults (as of 2020). According to a number of measures described later, they are more

de Pastoral Juvenil Hispana (La RED); National Federation for Catholic Youth Ministry; North American Forum for Small Christian Communities; RENEW; and Vietnamese Eucharistic Youth Movement.

active in the Church than other young adult Catholics and, as such, can be considered the future of the Church. For that matter, they already are the present.

The purpose of this chapter is to sketch a general portrait of young adult Catholics regularly involved in Small Christian Communities pre-pandemic (referred to as "SCC participants" from here on) as compared to their peers—other young adult Catholics not regularly involved in Small Christian Communities (called "non-participants" from here on). To this end, the following description provides sociodemographic characteristics (including gender, race/ethnicity, age, and stage in the life cycle), followed by the description of religiosity and motivations for participation in the communities. The chapter concludes with recommendations for how to engage more young adult Catholics in the Small Christian Communities in the United States.

The subject of Catholics' involvement in SCCs has been explored before. A number of publications described SCCs in the United States on a national level.[5] Some studies offered a more nuanced look at a particular group or movement[6] or a particular facet, such as the intersection of Small Christian Communities and parish life.[7]

---

[5] See Bernard Lee, *The Catholic Experience of Small Christian Communities*; Bernard Lee and Michael Cowan, "Priority Concerns of SCCs in American Catholicism," in Healey and Hinton, *Small Christian Communities Today: Capturing the New Moment*, 63–72; Massimo Faggioli, *Sorting Out Catholicism: A Brief History of the New Ecclesial Movements* (Collegeville, MN: Liturgical Press, 2014); and Julian Porteous, *A New Wine and Fresh Skins: Ecclesial Movements in the Church* (Cleveland, Australia: Modotti Press, 2010).

[6] See Pierre Hegy, *Wake Up, Lazarus!: On Catholic Renewal* (Self-published: iUniverse, 2012) for an exploration of Catholic Renewal and William D'Antonio, "Communitas Celebrating Twenty Years of Building Community," in Healey and Hinton, *Small Christian Communities Today: Capturing the New Moment*, 49–54, for an exploration of Communitas.

[7] See John Paul Vandenakker, *Small Christian Communities and the Parish: An Ecclesiological Analysis of the North American Experience* (Kansas City, MO: Sheed & Ward, 1994); Kenneth G. Davis, "Built from Living Stones: Hispanic

Unless stated differently, all the findings presented in this chapter come from three studies conducted by CARA between 2019 and 2021: the National Poll of Young Catholics, the National Survey of Small Christian Communities, and interviews with Catholics working with Small Christian Communities in the United States. Information about the methodology used in those studies can be found in the appendix.

Gender and Race/Ethnicity

Among US Catholics ages eighteen to thirty-five who regularly participated in Small Christian Communities pre-pandemic, approximately half were male (48%) and half (52%) were female. This is a similar proportion to that found among other Catholics in this age group.[8]

Beneath this surface level similarity, men and women differed in regard to which SCCs they joined and their motivations for joining them. For instance, men were *more* likely to participate in an associate community of a religious order or in a charismatic community (by 6 percentage points each). Women were 7 percentage points *more* likely to be "very much" motivated by a desire to nourish their spiritual lives.

Another way the SCC participants differed from non-participants has to do with their ethnic/racial background. In general, minorities were more likely than Whites to participate in SCCs. Specifically, only four in ten Whites participated in SCCs as compared to nine in ten Blacks and five in ten Hispanics, Asians, and others.[9]

Catholic Parishes Without Boundaries or Buildings," *New Blackfriars* 88, no. 1015 (2007): 335–52; and Susan DeGuide and Steven Valenzuela, "Development of SFCs in the Diocese of San Bernardio, California," in Healey and Hinton, *Small Christian Communities Today: Capturing the New Moment*, 41–48.

[8] The margin of error for these and the following statistics is ±3.2% (at 95% CL).

[9] Note that Blacks were the smallest of the distinguished minorities, both overall and among SCC participants. Specifically, Blacks constituted 7 percent

Blacks were not only the most likely to participate in SCCs; they also participated the most frequently. Specifically, 30 percent of Blacks participated on a weekly basis and 21 percent on bi-weekly basis as compared to 9 percent and 7 percent of all other races/ethnicities, respectively.

The reason why minorities are more likely than Whites to participate in SCCs seems not to be that minorities are more interested in joining those groups in bigger numbers, but rather that Whites are harder to engage. According to the interviewees who worked with SCCs around the world, Whites are more individualistic (as opposed to communal and family-centered), more agenda-driven, more focused on accomplishing things (as opposed to relationship-driven, focused on spending time with each other), more private (as opposed to willing to share their inner life with others), and more intellectual, sharing from their head (as opposed to being more natural, sharing from their heart).[10]

The individualistic nature of White young adult Catholics (as opposed to the more communitarian nature of minorities) makes it much harder to organize White-majority groups. While not all interviewees agreed on this point, some observed that Hispanic groups may be more diverse/inclusive due to their family orientation. This may mean that they are literally bringing their whole families to group meetings (as opposed to coming individually). Interviewees said, for example, that "the Hispanic groups are more age-inclusive, like they'll bring

---

of SCC participants as compared to Hispanics (44%), Whites (39%), Asians (7%), and others (3%). Additionally, Blacks constituted 4 percent of all young adult Catholics as compared to Whites (45%), Hispanics (43%), Asians (6%), and others (3%). On a methodological note, there were seventy-seven Blacks in the nationally representative dataset used for this analysis (sixty-seven were SCC participants and ten were not). For the sake of brevity, words "Hispanic" and "Latino"/"Latina" are used interchangeably.

[10] These cultural differences may be better described as not between White American-Europeans and ethnic/racial minorities, but between westerners who are sixty years old or younger and others.

their kids to it" and that there is "a lot more diversity in the Hispanic community, which makes it for them very multi-cultural from the Hispanic point of view."

Whites are more agenda-driven, more focused on accomplishing things (as opposed to relationship-driven, focused on spending time with each other). In practice, this means that White majority groups often prefer to meet for a pre-determined period (e.g., Advent) and pre-determined (and often shorter) amount of time. On the other hand, rather than meeting for a pre-determined amount of time (to complete a set agenda, such as Bible study or prayers), minority groups meet for a longer time (often, as long as there is food and company of others available). One interviewee described it in the following way:

> *White European, I think, there's an efficiency model. We have a task to do. So, we're going to do some small talk for, like, five minutes but they already get right to it. That type of desire to get to the task supersedes the pleasantries, supersedes the relational fraternal communion that's being fostered. And so therefore, I would say that in the White European communities, I think that . . . there's a greater awareness . . . that they're there for a purpose. And this is the purpose and we have to do that purpose. I don't necessarily sense that from some of the other cultural communities where the idea of accompaniment and relationship is of higher value than the functionality of a small group. If we don't even get to the Bible study that we're meant to talk about, so be it. We learned about each other. And so, I think that . . . because of that, the strength of the rootedness of those conversations I feel is stronger and lasts longer. . . . I see many young adult groups say, we're going to do a six-week series for Lent. And they emphasize the six-week series. You only have to do this for six-weeks, so there's an efficiency to it. It's almost perceived as the time sacrifice. . . . All you got to worry about is just six weeks. Six weeks you can be done with us. That type of tone is not as prevalent in Hispanic Latino communities, in African American communities. I think that is the difference. So, yeah, I think that's a dynamic that's very different. I don't know if it's good or bad; it is different, though.*

Another cultural difference has to do with how Whites approach SCCs more intellectually, sharing from their head (as opposed to being more natural, sharing from their heart). For example, Whites tend to "look more for the intellectual approach of the small communities and . . . look more to know the doctrine instead to live the faith." On the other hand, minorities may be more inclined to "believe that small communities are the way to live the faith, [they seek to live out] the sense of solidarity and the sense of communion, the sense of fraternity."

Whites also tend to be more private (as opposed to freely sharing their inner life with others). One of the interviewees described how this private mindset interferes with the process of engaging in communities:

> I asked a Catholic sister who coordinated the Small Christian Communities in New Jersey. And I asked her, what's the biggest obstacle when you're forming these Small Christian Communities in these middle-class parishes? And her answer was shocking to me. Fear. Fear. She said, 'People don't want to be vulnerable to their neighbors, to share their weaknesses.' I mean, weaknesses may be divorce, alcoholism, a child on drug abuse. They don't like to do that, and they feel that if they're pressured into these Small Christian Communities, people are sharing what we call their vulnerability and their weaknesses. She said that, for many middle-class Whites, they want to avoid that.

Finally, minorities seem more likely to notice and be subjected to racism that may affect their engagement in the Church and participation in SCCs. Hispanic interviewees stated that racism is prevalent in society and in the Church specifically and that it can be accompanied (or replaced) by colorism, classism, and/or religious discrimination. They pointed out that racism often becomes a black-and-white issue, leaving Hispanics out. Some Hispanics tend to treat this situation as a fact of life and are not inclined to discuss or address it.

From the organizational perspective, some of the interviewees indicated that SCCs often see themselves as a venue for learning about God, for acting upon Biblically mandated issues (e.g., feeding the hungry), and for pro-life activism but not for much else (thus leaving out issues such as racism). On the other hand, other interviewees provided a number of examples ranging from local parish communities to national Catholic organizations that encourage discussion and action on racial justice. Based on their comments, overall, the church, as a body of faithful, appears to be increasingly aware and active in this area. However, the Catholic Church hierarchy is viewed as largely missing from those efforts. The next chapter explores these issues of gender and ethnicity in more detail.

Age and Life Cycle

US Catholics ages eighteen to thirty-five who regularly participated in Small Christian Communities pre-pandemic were younger (both in terms of age and stage in life cycle) than other Catholics in this age group. Specifically, SCC participants were, on average, two years younger than non-participants in the eighteen to thirty-five age group. The age of participants depended, in some cases, on the type of SCC. For instance, young adult Catholics involved in college student communities (e.g., a Newman Center) and those participating in weekend retreats (e.g., Cursillo or its derivatives, like Teens Encounter Christ) were two years *younger*, on average, than other young adult Catholics. Similarly, those participating in Bible study communities, choirs, and rosary circles were one year *younger*, on average.

Perhaps more insightful than the absolute age are milestones in a person's life cycle. As compared to non-participants, the SCC participants were 11 percentage points *more* likely to be still living with their parents, 3 percentage points *less* likely to be living alone, 6 percentage points *less* likely to be living with a spouse or a partner, and 3 percentage points *less* likely to be already living with a spouse or a partner *and* their own children. While education is not as good an approximation of one's stage in the life cycle, it shows a similar pattern. As compared to non-participants, the SCC participants were 5 percentage points *more* likely to have a high school education or less and 6 percentage points *less* likely to have a college education or more.

Among those involved in Small Christian Communities, young adult Catholic SCCs differed in some substantial ways from older Catholic SCCs. From an organizational perspective, young adult SCCs[11] tend to have a more established meeting format, leadership structure, and articulated charism, spirituality, purpose, or mission. Less than half had an established leadership selection process, budget, and written policies. And less than a quarter had a legal status and experience receiving grants.

Religiosity

Overall, US Catholics ages eighteen to thirty-five who regularly participated in Small Christian Communities pre-pandemic were *more* likely than non-participants to report more Catholic elements in their upbringing, as well as higher levels of organizational, non-organizational, and intrinsic religiosity, as defined below.

The SCC participants exhibited *more* Catholic elements during their upbringing. For example, as compared to non-participants, SCC participants were *more* likely to have attended a Catholic elementary, middle, or junior high school (by 14

---

[11] In CARA's study, these young adult SCCs are defined as groups located in the United States, that have at least some Catholic members, that self-identified as a youth group, high school, or college group, and/or that report that at least half of their members are under thirty-five years old.

percentage points), a Catholic high school (by 12 percentage points), or a Catholic college or university (by 9 percentage points). While growing up, they were also *more* likely to have participated in a parish-based Catholic religious education program for youth (by 10 percentage points), a parish youth group (by 9 percentage points), Catholic campus ministry on a college or university campus (by 8 percentage points), or scouting groups (by 6 percentage points). In addition, they were more likely to be intentional about being Catholic, as they were 13 percentage points *less* likely than non-participants to be cradle Catholics. In other words, SCC participants were more likely to have actively decided to become Catholic as children, teenagers, or young adults.

SCC participants showed higher levels of *organizational religious activity*, which can be defined as "public religious activities such as attending religious services or participating in other group-related religious activity"[12]. For instance, SCC participants attended Mass *more* frequently than non-participants. Specifically, SCC participants were *more* likely to attend Mass weekly (by 11 percentage points), almost weekly (by 8 percentage points), or once/twice a month (by 7 percentage points). On the other side, the non-participants were *more* likely to attend Mass a few times a year (by 5 percentage points) or even less regularly/never (by 23 percentage points).

SCC participants showed higher levels of *non-organizational religious activity*, which can be defined as consisting "of religious activities performed in private, such as prayer, scripture study, watching religious TV or listening to religious radio."[13] As compared to non-participants, SCC participants were *more* likely to pray individually (outside of Mass) daily or more

---

[12] Harold G. Koenig and Arndt Büssing, "The Duke University Religion Index (DUREL): A Five-Item Measure for Use in Epidemological Studies," *Religions* 1, no. 1 (2010): 78–85.

[13] Koenig and Büssing, 80.

often (by 12 percentage points), *more* than once a week (by 3 percentage points), once a week (by 3 percentage points), and almost every week (by 3 percentage points). On the other hand, non-participants were *more* likely to pray individually a few times a year only (by 7 percentage points) or rarely/never (by 16 percentage points). The non-participants were also *more* likely to rarely/never pray with their family (by 33 percentage points) and people outside their family (by 41 percentage points).

SCC participants showed higher levels of *intrinsic religiosity*, which can be defined as a "degree of personal religious commitment or motivation."[14] For instance, SCC participants were 16 percentage points *more* likely to be registered with a Catholic parish. A description of the motivations for participating in SCCs can be found in the following section.

Motivations

As noted at the beginning, for the purpose of this chapter, Small Christian Communities are defined as Catholic groups or communities of people meeting to practice their faith (e.g., Bible study, prayer, devotions, faith sharing), to provide service or assistance to others, and/or to evangelize and spread their faith to others. As such, participation in SCCs can be conceptualized as a form of volunteering, and SCC participants can be seen as volunteers.

In their review of academic literature on volunteering, Musick and Wilson stated that "[t]he best-known and most sophisticated psychological theory of volunteer motivations takes a functional approach."[15] The specific functional motivations that volunteers want to address vary between different

---

[14] Koenig and Büssing, 80.
[15] Mark A. Musick and John Wilson, *Volunteers: A Social Profile* (Bloomington, IN: Indiana University Press, 2007), 56.

industries.[16] Regardless of the industry, all functional motivations can be compiled into a single list. Clary et al. distinguish six functional motivations: to improve career opportunities (i.e., career motivation), to develop and strengthen social relationships (i.e., social motivation), to act or express important convictions concerning serving others (i.e., values motivation), to learn from new experiences (i.e., understand motivation), to increase positive feelings and develop ego (i.e., enhancement motivation), and to reduce negative feelings and protect ego (i.e., protect motivation).[17] Each of these motivations is described below.

The most prevalent functional motivation for why young adult Catholics got involved in SCCs was the desire to learn from new experiences (i.e., the understand motivation). Specifically, seven in ten SCC participants stated that they were motivated "somewhat" or "very much" by a desire to learn from new experiences (74% of SCC participants). Furthermore, half of SCC participants were motivated by a desire to explore different religious traditions (48% of SCC participants).

The second most common functional motivation among SCC participants is the desire to enhance ego and increase positive feelings (i.e., the enhancement motivation). Current literature finds evidence of this relationship for various populations. For example, Sokolowski analyzed 2,671 responses from a national random survey conducted in 1992 and found that a desire for self-improvement had an effect on the amount of volunteering.[18] Jenner conducted a survey of 292 active

---

[16] Lewis M. Segal and Burton A. Weisbrod, "Volunteer Labor Sorting Across Industries," *Journal of Policy Analysis and Management* 21 (2002): 427–47.

[17] E. Gil Clary et al., "Understanding and assessing the motivations of volunteers: A functional approach," *Journal of Personality and Social Psychology* 74, no. 6 (1998): 1516–30.

[18] S. Wojciech Sokolowski, "Show me the way to the next worthy deed: Towards a microstructural theory of volunteering and giving," *Voluntas* 7 (1996): 259–78.

members of a national women's volunteer organization between eighteen and forty-two years old.[19] She found that some
respondents were motivated by a desire for self-actualization.
In the CARA study that forms the basis for this book, a relatively high number—seven in ten young adult Catholics—was
motivated by a desire to nourish their spiritual life (70% of
SCC participants).
Current literature also shows that individuals may choose
to volunteer to reduce negative feelings (i.e., the protective
motivation). For example, Musick and Wilson found, for
people over sixty-five nationally, that volunteering lowers
depression levels and that volunteering for religious causes
has a stronger effect on depression levels than volunteering
for secular causes.[20] Blackstone conducted field research at an
affiliate office of the Komen Breast Cancer Foundation and
found that many women volunteered to connect with other
women and to share the common experience of a breast cancer
diagnosis.[21] In this CARA study, seven in ten SCC participants
were motivated by a desire to reduce negative feelings (69%
of SCC participants).
Some volunteers may be driven by a desire to develop and
strengthen social ties (i.e., the social motivation). For example,
Toppe, Kirsch, and Michel examined 4,216 responses from a
nationally representative sample of adult Americans and found
that 66 percent of volunteers considered meeting new people

---

[19] Jessica R. Jenner, "Participation, leadership, and the role of volunteerism
among selected women volunteers," *Journal of Voluntary Action Research* 11,
no. 4 (1982): 27–38.

[20] Mark A. Musick and John Wilson, "Volunteering and depression: The
role of psychological and social resources in different age groups," *Social
Science & Medicine* 56, no. 2 (2003): 259–69.

[21] Amy Blackstone, " 'It's just about being fair': Activism and the politics
of volunteering in the breast cancer movement," *Gender & Society* 18, no. 3
(2004): 350–68.

to be an important reason for volunteering.[22] A study based on a telephone survey of 1,001 respondents in Illinois found that the third most frequently cited reason for volunteering, reported by 74 percent of volunteers, was the motivation to work with people who share the volunteers' ideals.[23] In the CARA study, two in three SCC participants were motivated by a desire to develop and strengthen social ties with others (65% of SCC participants). Unsurprisingly, the share of people exhibiting this motivation increased with the frequency of their attendance at the SCC: 19 percent of those who attended SCCs once a year were very motivated by the desire to develop and strengthen social ties with others, as compared to 23 percent of those attending once a month, 27 percent of those attending once every three weeks, 33 percent of those attending once every two weeks, 43 percent of those attending every week, and 51 percent of those attending more than once a week.

Another functional motivation that may be related to participation in SCCs is the desire to act or express important convictions concerning serving others (i.e., the values motivation). Past research tends to indicate that higher values motivation is positively related to volunteering. For example, Toppe, Kirsch, and Michel examined 4,216 responses from a nationally representative sample of adult Americans and found that 96 percent of all volunteers (and 98% of volunteers to religious organizations) considered compassion towards others to be an important reason for volunteering, while 90 percent of volunteers considered helping those who have less to be an

[22] Christopher M. Toppe, Arthur D. Kirsch, and Jocabel Michel, *Giving and volunteering in the United States: Findings from a national survey, 2001 Edition* (Washington, DC: Independent Sector, 2001).

[23] Richard Schuldt et al., *Profile of Illinois: An Engaged State. Illinois Civic Engagement Benchmark Survey Results* (Springfield, IL: Illinois Civic Engagement Project, 2001).

important reason for volunteering.[24] In CARA's study, three in five SCC participants were motivated at least "somewhat" by a desire to act or express important convictions concerning serving others (58% of SCC participants). Finally, individuals may also volunteer out of utilitarian motives. For instance, Cugno and Ferrero conceptualized volunteering as a selfish and rational investment.[25] Musick and Wilson note, "Although some might feel uncomfortable citing work-related motivations for volunteering, it is quite common for schools, colleges, and volunteer agencies to tout this as a reason for doing volunteer work."[26] Previous studies are not consistent in their assessment of the role of utilitarian motives in volunteering. For example, Sokolowski found that the desire to advance one's career did not have an observable effect on the amount of volunteering.[27] On the other hand, Jenner found that women were equally motivated by altruism and self-actualization.[28] In CARA's study, half of SCC participants were motivated at least "somewhat" by a desire to improve career opportunities (i.e., the career motivation) (54% of SCC participants). The share of people exhibiting this motivation increased with the frequency of attendance: 20 percent of those who attended SCCs once a month or less often were very motivated by the desire to improve career opportunities, as compared to 27 percent of those attending once every three weeks, 30 percent of those attending once every two weeks, 35 percent of those attending every week, and 38 percent of those attending more than once a week.

[24] Toppe, Kirsch, and Michel, *Giving and volunteering in the United States.*

[25] Franco Cugno and Mario Ferrero, "Competition among volunteers," *European Journal of Political Economy* 20, no. 3 (2004): 637–54.

[26] Musick and Wilson, *Volunteers: A Social Profile,* 61.

[27] Sokolowski, "Show me the way."

[28] Jenner, "Participation, leadership."

Implications and Recommendations

The findings described above provide a general sketch of young adult Catholics regularly involved in Small Christian Communities. These findings also hint at some of the challenges and opportunities that the Church is facing as it seeks to make parish life relevant to younger generations. The following description summarizes some implications of the findings as well as recommendations from interviews that CARA conducted with fourteen English-speaking and eight Spanish-speaking Catholics working with Small Christian Communities in the United States (including pastors, religious sisters, university professors/researchers, parish and diocesan staff members, and leaders of national and international umbrella organizations fostering Small Christian Communities in the Catholic Church, in particular youth groups, campus groups, young adult groups, and Hispanic/Latino groups).

Recruit More Paid Staff and Volunteer Leaders

Some interviewees observed that the growth of SCCs is limited by the availability of volunteer group leaders, especially in environments such as campus ministry where there is constant turnover. One of the interviewees working at a university-based parish stated that he could have as many groups as he has young adult leaders available. Another one said that "[p]eople want to meet in communities, but nobody wants to lead." These communities need people who "are prepared to lead, have the charism to lead, who are open, who have the space in their homes, etc." Another interviewee added a caveat that putting young adults in leadership positions should be a carefully paced process. She said that "young people have to feel . . . that they're not going to put expectations on them before they are ready to say yes."

Overall, volunteer leaders are very important to growing SCCs, but they cannot fully replace trained, experienced, and specialized paid personnel (in parishes and dioceses). A major challenge related to attracting more people to these groups is the limited availability of such personnel due to insufficient funds. A few interviewees noted that funding was reduced as a consequence of broader budget cuts resulting from the mounting costs of sexual abuse cases. One interviewee observed that, in some places, "people don't have money to pay for a full-time youth minister in the parish . . . with the payouts from the sexual abuse cases."

More recently, during the financial crises in parishes caused by the pandemic, SCC coordinators were among the first staff members to be laid off. Interviewees believe that this has had major negative consequences during the pandemic (at a time when young Catholics need SCCs more than usual) and in the future (because the decrease in SCCs may lead to a decrease in the number of future Church vocations).

Enlist Support from Pastors (and Bishops)

A few interviewees described a general lack of involvement or, in some cases, a negative influence of pastors on the proliferation of SCCs in parishes. Interviewees believe that this situation developed over the last two decades (i.e., between 2000 and 2020) and may be related to the shortage of priests, to pastors not realizing the beneficial potential of SCCs, to pastors being more controlling than before, and to pastors being weary of SCCs after the sexual abuse scandals. Some interviewees postulated that greater support from pastors, as well as bishops, is needed to make SCCs more central to Church life.

Bolster Small Groups through Big Events

A few interviewees observed that, currently, instead of complementing each other, big events (such as World Youth Day, national gatherings of FOCUS and NCYC, and parish festivals) and SCCs often act as substitutes that are competing for limited resources. However, SCCs and big events have different purposes: SCCs are about building high-quality relationships, while big events are about growing high numbers of participants. When approached with intentionality, they may complement each other. Specifically, big events bring more people into the Church and bring new energy that comes with large gatherings. This can be utilized to form new SCCs and to continue currently existing SCCs.

Listen to Young People, Support Them, and Give Them Agency

Interviewees observed that the Church needs to listen to young people, both on the institutional level and the human level. The Church needs to meet them where they are (rather than waiting for them in the parish), reach out to them (rather than waiting for them to make the contact), give them space to talk about things important to them, accompany them in their suffering and struggles, make them feel accepted, affirm them, and encourage them (as opposed to laying "on them burdens and regulations"). Some interviewees observed how the pandemic intensified problems of young people (e.g., loneliness and problems with unemployment) and that this is a particularly important time for the Church to listen to and to support young adults. Some interviewees postulated that young people need to be leaders both in their own ministry (with support from adult leaders) and in the Church in general (e.g., by being invited to parish councils) because they are the ones in touch with the culture of their peers and they are the present and the future of the Church. These observations echo findings and postulates from other studies. For instance, fifteen years earlier, Lee and Cowan wrote that "[w]e need to learn how to welcome youth and young adults into Small Christian Communities."[29]

---

[29] Lee and Cowan, "Priority Concerns of SCCs," 68.

Address Hypocrisy and Inauthenticity in the Church

Several interviewees observed that engaging young people in SCCs is made difficult by hypocrisy and inauthenticity in the Church (whether real or perceived). From the perspective of some people, the Church appears silent on its own shortcomings (e.g., sexual abuse, racism, judgementalism, and gossip). There appears to be a disconnect between what the Church teaches and how the Church acts, both as a hierarchy and as a body of the faithful. Interviewees postulate that the Church needs to create safe venues for exploring, discussing, and addressing those issues with young people.

Reach Out to Progressive Types

One interviewee observed that, currently, SCCs tend to attract more conservative Catholics while young people overall tend to be more progressive. Thus, there is a need to reach out more to the progressive types. This may mean incorporating more discussion (and activities) focusing on social issues at the forefront of mainstream society (e.g., LBGTQ advocacy and support, climate justice, and racial justice). It may also mean exploring and addressing the discrepancy between the Church's teaching and mainstream practices among young adults, such as cohabiting before marriage.

Recognize Different Needs of People from Different Cultural Backgrounds

As will be noted in the next chapter, different races/ethnicities engage in SCCs differently and for different reasons. Interviewees confirmed those findings and observed that SCCs need to be sensitive to the needs of different races/ethnicities if they want to attract more young people from different demographics. Again, these postulates are not new and echo previous studies. For instance, Lee and Cowan wrote that "[w]e need to forge a much better relationship, a partnership of equals, between Hispanic/Latino and Anglo SCCs."[30]

Develop Models for Online Meetings

In most places, the pandemic led to suspension of group meetings or to a switch from an in-person to online format (e.g., over Zoom, Facebook, or WhatsApp). This switch created a number of opportunities as well as challenges, with some places and demographics being better suited than others to make the transition.

Some of the opportunities identified in the interviews include the ease of access and the removal of geographic limitations on who can participate in online meetings (allowing for easier participation by, for example, people with disabilities, people who are sick, people without access to transportation, people living in different parts of the world, and people of different backgrounds).

On the other hand, some of the challenges related to online meetings include "screen fatigue," the lack of the "experience" that in-person meetings offer (something that may be a bigger issue for Hispanics than for primarily White groups), a risk of shifting the focus from creating quality relationships to pursuing higher numbers of participants, and problems with technology (e.g., reliability of internet connection, access to internet-enabled devices, and ability to operate these devices).

Of course, the growth in importance of online meetings is not the only consequence of the pandemic lockdown. See Chapter 7 for further exploration of where to minister to young adult Catholics in the post-pandemic world.

[30] Lee and Cowan, 65.

CHAPTER THREE

The Role of Small Christian Communities for Catholic Young Adults: Differences by Gender and Ethnicity

Patricia Wittberg, SC

Introduction

As was noted in the introduction to this book, recent studies uniformly agree that young adults in North America today are less likely than preceding generations to identify with any established religion and more likely to be religious "nones."[1]

---

[1] See Christian Smith and Patricia Snell, *Souls in Transition: The Religious and Spiritual Lives of Emerging Adults* (New York: Oxford University Press, 2009); Pew Forum on Religion and Public Life, *'Nones' on the Rise: One-In-Five Adults Have No Religious Affiliation* (Washington, DC: Pew Research Center, 2012); Pew Research Center, "In U.S., Decline of Christianity Continues at a Rapid Pace," October 17, 2019, https://www.pewforum.org/2019/10/17/in-u-s-decline-of-christianity-continues-at-rapid-pace/; Melissa Chan, Kim M. Tsai, and Andrew Fuligni, "Changes in Religiosity across the Transition to Young Adulthood," *Journal of Youth and Adolescence* 44, no. 8 (2015): 1555–66; Joel Thiessen and Sarah Wilkins-LaFlamme, "Becoming a Religious None: Irreligious Socialization and Disaffiliation," *Journal for the Scientific Study of Religion* 56, no. 1 (2017): 64–82; Joel Thiessen and Sarah Wilkins-LaFlamme, *None of the Above: Non-Religious Identity in the U.S. and Canada* (New York: New York University Press, 2020); Vern L. Bengtson et al., "Bringing Up Nones: Intergenerational Influences and Cohort Trends," *Journal for the Scientific Study of Religion* 57, no. 2 (2018): 258–76; Tim Clydesdale and Kathleen Garces-Foley, *The Twenty-Something Soul: Understanding the Religious and Secular Lives of*

They are also less likely to hold orthodox beliefs about religious doctrines and moral issues.[2] Their religious practice has progressively declined, both in attendance at weekly denominational services and in celebrating lifestyle transition rituals such as baptisms, marriages, and funerals.[3]

American Young Adults (New York: Oxford University Press, 2019); Melinda Lundquist Denton and Richard Flory, *Back-Pocket God: Religion and Spirituality in the Lives of Emerging Adults* (New York: Oxford University Press, 2020); and Dennis Sadowski, "Poll finds church membership continues downward trend in the 21st century," *Catholic News Service*, March 31, 2021, https://www .catholicsun.org/2021/03/31/poll-finds-church-membership-continues -downward-trend-in-21st-century/.

[2] See William V. D'Antonio et al., *American Catholics: Gender, Generation, and Commitment* (Lanham, MD: Rowman and Littlefield, 2001); William V. D'Antonio et al., *American Catholics Today: New Realities of Their Faith and Their Church* (Lanham, MD: Rowman and Littlefield, 2007); Christian Smith and Patricia Snell, *Souls in Transition*; Justin Farrell, "The Young and the Restless? The Liberation of Young Evangelicals," *Journal for the Scientific Study of Religion* 50, no. 3 (2011): 517–32; Phillip R. Hardy, Kelly L. Kandra, and Brian G. Patterson, *Joy and Grievance in an American Diocese* (Lisle, IL: Benedictine University, 2014); Keith A. Puffer, "Protestant Millennials, Religious Doubt, and the Local Church," *Religions* 9, no. 8 (2017); Jean M. Twenge, *iGen: Why Today's Super-Connected Kids Are Growing Up Less Rebellious, More Tolerant, Less Happy—And Completely Unprepared for Adulthood* (New York: Atria Books, 2017); Douglas Jacobs et al., "Adventist Millennials: Measuring Emerging Adults' Connection to Church," *Review of Religious Research* 61, no. 1 (2019): 39–56; and Pew Research Center, "In U.S., Decline of Christianity Continues at a Rapid Pace."

[3] See Smith and Snell, *Souls in Transition*; Mark M. Gray, "Exclusive Analysis: National Catholic Marriage Rate Plummets," *Our Sunday Visitor*, June 26, 2011, http://www.osv.com/tabid/7621/itemid/8053/Exclusive-analysis-National-Catholic-marriage-rat.aspx (site discontinued); Center for Applied Research in the Apostolate, "Declining Proportion of Baptisms a Cause for Concern," *The CARA Report* 19, no. 1 (2013): 3; Christian Smith et al., *Young Catholic America: Emerging Adults In, Out of, and Gone from the Church* (New York: Oxford University Press, 2014); Jean M. Twenge et al., "Generational and Time Period Differences in American Adolescents' Religious Orientation, 1966–2014," *Public Library of Science ONE* 10, no. 5 (2015), e0121454; Puffer, "Protestant Millennials"; Linda Woodhead, "The Rise of 'No Religion': Towards an Explanation," *Sociology of Religion* 78, no. 3 (2017): 247–62; Bob Smietana, "Why No One May Be Getting Married at Your Church This

Nor do young adults seem to be returning to religious practice as they get older.[4] Disaffiliation appears to be especially pronounced among women. A succession of studies over the past twenty-five years has found that, contrary to longstanding historical patterns, young adult Catholic women are now less observant in their attendance, less orthodox in their beliefs, and less likely to remain Catholic than young adult Catholic males are.[5] This trend appears recently to have spread to other faith traditions, where the youngest women are more likely than men to report never attending religious services.[6] Overall, close to a fifth of American congregations now report having no young adults at all in their church, more than double the percentage that did so in 2010.[7]

This religious disaffiliation is not universal among all young adults, however. A minority of youth have become more religiously observant, devout, and orthodox than the rest of their

---

Summer," *Facts and Trends*, May 31, 2018, https://research.lifeway.com/2018/05/31/why-no-one-may-be-getting-married-at-your-church-this-summer/; Samuel L. Perry and Kyle C. Longest, "Examining the Impact of Religious Initiation Rites on Religiosity and Disaffiliation over Time," *Journal for the Scientific Study of Religion* 58, no. 4 (2019): 891–904; and Stephen Bullivant, *Mass Exodus: Catholic Disaffiliation in Britain and America since Vatican II* (New York: Oxford University Press, 2019).

[4] See Michael Hout and Claude S. Fischer, "Explaining Why More Americans Have No Religious Preference: Political Backlash and Generational Succession, 1987–2012," *Sociological Science* 1 (2014): 423–46; Jones et al., *Exodus: Why Americans Are Leaving Religion*; and Denton and Flory, *Back-Pocket God*.

[5] See James D. Davidson et al., *The Search for Common Ground: What Unites and Divides Catholic Americans* (Huntington, IN: Our Sunday Visitor Press, 1997), and William V. D'Antonio, Michele Dillon, and Mary L. Gautier, *American Catholics in Transition* (Lanham, MD: Rowman and Littlefield, 2013).

[6] See Pew Research Center, "In U.S., Decline of Christianity Continues at a Rapid Pace," and Guy Bruge, "Behind the Steep Decline in Church Attendance among Women," *State of the Church* (blog), *Barna Group*, March 4, 2020, https://www.barna.com/?s=Behind+the+steep+decline+in+church+attendance+among+women.

[7] Jacobs et al., "Adventist Millennials."

generation. Depending on the characteristics used to classify young adults as "religiously active," authors have estimated them to comprise as few as 8 percent[8] or as many as 15 percent[9] of their age group. This most religiously active segment—proudly orthodox and often aggressively evangelistic—has been separately studied by several researchers and extensively profiled by the media, which may make them appear to be a larger proportion of their generation than they actually are.[10] The question of whether this orthodox minority is the forerunner of a future revival of church membership or an indicator of organized religion's relegation to an irrelevancy and marginalization is of obvious importance to US denominations in general and to the US Catholic Church in particular.

Until now, US Catholicism has been somewhat shielded from declining membership by the in-migration of Catholics from other parts of the world. Hispanics have accounted for 71 percent of the overall growth in Catholicism in the United States since 1960.[11] Today, some 34 percent of US Catholics are Hispanic.[12] Among the youngest generation of Catholic adults,

---

[8] Kendra Creasy Dean, *Almost Christian: What the Faith of Our Teenagers Is Telling the American Church* (New York: Oxford University Press, 2010).

[9] Smith and Snell, *Souls in Transition*.

[10] See Colleen Carroll, *The New Faithful: Why Young Adults Are Embracing Orthodoxy* (Chicago: Loyola University Press, 2004); Smith and Snell, *Souls in Transition*; John P. Hoffman, "Declining Religious Authority? Confidence in the Leaders of Religious Organizations, 1973–2010," *Review of Religious Research* 55, no. 1 (2013): 1–25; Puffer, "Protestant Millennials"; Emily DeRogatis, *Saving Sex: Sexuality and Salvation in American Evangelicalism* (New York: Oxford University Press, 2015); and Katherine Dugan, *Millennial Missionaries: How a Group of Young Catholics Is Trying to Make Catholicism Cool* (New York: Oxford University Press, 2019).

[11] Mark M. Gray, "Exclusive Analysis: National Catholic Marriage Rate Plummets," *Our Sunday Visitor*, June 26, 2011.

[12] Frank Newport, "An Update on Catholics in the U.S.," *Gallup*, August 21, 2018, https://news.gallup.com/opinion/polling-matters/241235/update -catholics.aspx.

the Hispanic percentage approaches 50 percent.[13] But the children and grandchildren of Hispanic immigrants do not always *remain* Catholic. In 2010, 63 percent of Hispanic adults in the US self-identified as Catholic. Only 54 percent did so in 2016.[14] These are overall figures; the percentage of Catholics is even lower among some nationality groups such as Guatemalan immigrants or Puerto Ricans.

The rate of leaving Catholicism increases the longer Hispanics have lived in this country. One poll found that, while 61 percent of Hispanics born outside the US identify as Catholics, only half of those born in this country do so. Of those who leave Catholicism, half join conservative Protestant churches, and another quarter drop out of religion altogether.[15] Hispanic young adults are the least likely to remain Catholic and the most likely to claim that they have no religion at all.[16] And those who do remain in the Catholic Church are significantly less likely to say they are very religious (43%), as compared to Hispanics who are Protestant (60%).[17] A similar attenuation has been observed among the children and grandchildren of Catholic immigrants from other parts of the world.[18]

---

[13] Mark M. Gray, "A Dip in the Adult Catholic Population," *Nineteen Sixty-four* (blog), *Center for Applied Research in the Apostolate*, March 12, 2018, http://nineteensixty-four.blogspot.com/2018/03/a-dip-in-adult-catholic-population.html.

[14] Gray, "Dip in the Adult Catholic Population."

[15] Baylor Institute for Studies of Religion, "Current Research," *Religion Watch* 29, no. 6 (2014).

[16] Frank Newport, "U.S. Catholic Population: Less Religious, Shrinking," *Gallup*, February 25, 2013, http://www.gallup.com/poll/160691 (site discontinued).

[17] Newport, "U.S. Catholic Population," and Elizabeth Podrebarac Sciupac, "Hispanic Teens Enjoy Religious Activities with Parents, but Fewer View Religion as 'Very Important,'" *Pew Research Center*, September 22, 2020, https://www.pewresearch.org/fact-tank/2020/09/22/hispanic-teens-enjoy-religious-activities-with-parents-but-fewer-view-religion-as-very-important/.

[18] Stephen Kim, *Memory and Honor: Cultural and Generational Ministry with Korean American Communities* (Collegeville, MN: Liturgical Press, 2010).

This chapter addresses the light that the current CARA studies shed on the intersection of these trends and their implication for US Catholicism in the future. Specifically,

- To what extent and in what ways do Hispanic Catholics connect with religious practices in the United States? Are these similar to or different from the ways non-Hispanic Catholics connect? What are the implications for the Church in this country? For Hispanic Catholics?

- The gap between men and women in religious practice has declined or even vanished among non-Hispanic young adults. By some measures, non-Hispanic women are less religious than non-Hispanic men, reversing the earlier pattern in which women were much more religious. To what extent is this replicated among Catholic Hispanic young adults?

These questions are important because Hispanic young adult Catholics are rapidly becoming the majority among the US Catholics in their age group. The future of Catholicism in this country obviously depends on whether and how the youngest generation of Catholic men and women, Hispanic and non-Hispanic, remain attached to their faith.

Methodology

As is described in the Methodological Appendix, this chapter is based on two surveys: a National Survey of Young Catholics and a second National Survey of Small Christian Communities. The page numbers in this chapter refer to the page numbers in CARA's final report on this study.[19] In addi-

---

[19] Mark M. Gray, Michal J. Kramarek, and Thomas Gaunt, *Faith and Spiritual Life of Catholics in the United States*, Center for Applied Research in the Apostolate, February 2021.

tion, quotations are included from twenty-two interviews with persons actively working with Small Christian Communities in the United States. For a more detailed description of the methodology, please see the appendix.

Findings

Membership in Small Christian Communities

The survey of young Catholic adults shows that one of the strongest predictors of how actively connected the respondents in the present survey are with their faith is whether they participate in some sort of Small Christian Community (SCC). Approximately 45 percent of those surveyed have participated in at least one Catholic group or community of people meeting to practice their faith (e.g., Bible study, prayer, devotions, and faith sharing), to provide service or assistance to others, and/or to evangelize and spread their faith. Members of such groups or communities stand out in numerous ways. As the CARA study has already reported, those with high SCC membership are more likely to:

- Be registered in a parish

- Attend Mass weekly or more

- Have attended Catholic schools at an elementary, secondary, or post-secondary level

- Wear religious symbols and have them in their homes

- Pray privately and go to confession

- Participate in Eucharistic Adoration

- Be active in parish activities and ministries

And as Chapter 1 notes, members of Small Christian Communities are also more likely to struggle with their faith—which indicates that it is important enough to them to bother doing so, since they are also more likely to say they could never imagine themselves leaving the Catholic Church. Non-Hispanic young adults are less likely to belong to SCCs than older Catholics, and they are correspondingly less likely to score highly on any of the practices mentioned above. Among the Hispanic respondents, the pattern is different. The Hispanic respondents overall are significantly *more* likely to be involved in Small Christian Communities. They are also more likely to wear religious symbols and display religious items in their home, and to attend non-Mass religious celebrations such as the Day of the Dead or *quinceañeras*. But they are *less* likely to report having gone either to Catholic schools or to Catholic religious education. They are also less likely to be registered in a parish, and they report having fewer struggles with their faith. They are neither significantly more nor less likely to attend Mass, go to confession or Eucharistic Adoration, go on retreats, or be active in parish ministries than the non-Hispanic respondents are, in spite of their greater involvement in SCCs. Participation in Small Christian Communities, therefore, does not seem to have the same impact on Hispanic religious practice and connection to US Catholicism—at least on the dimensions of religious practice measured in this study—as it did on the religious practice and connection of non-Hispanics.

Why might this be the case? Hispanic SCCs, while larger than the non-Hispanic groups, are less likely to be connected with their local parish and more likely to meet in a member's home or in some other location. They are also more likely to gain new members through familial connections rather than through some sort of established, parish-based recruitment method. Their members are more likely to be married with children. Members of Hispanic SCCs are more likely than members of non-Hispanic ones to say that the best part of being a member is that it helps them improve their marriage and family life, that it is a gift of the Holy Spirit, and that it engages them in outreach. "Reducing negative feelings" is also cited by significantly more Hispanic respondents as a motivation for participating in SCCs. In contrast, while relatively few (8%) of the respondents overall say that they find their group's relationship with the parish to be challenging, the respondents in the Hispanic groups are significantly more likely (19% as compared to 7%) to feel this way.

Membership in SCCs, therefore, seems to serve a somewhat different function in Hispanic Catholicism (and perhaps in other new immigrant communities) than it does for non-Hispanic Catholics in the United States. For the former, it seems to help them and their families preserve important elements of the faith from their homelands in the face of a strange and overpowering American culture. It thus preserves a "domus Catholicism" that differs from the parish-centered Catholicism prevalent in the United States, as Allan Deck describes in Chapter 5.

A key question, therefore, is whether this function of Small Christian Communities will continue as the children and grandchildren of the first generation of Hispanics assimilate into the larger American culture. The survey's youngest Hispanic respondents (ages 18-20) are less likely than the older Hispanic respondents (ages 30-35) to consider themselves practicing Catholics and more likely to say that they are not religious persons. In this, they are beginning to resemble non-Hispanics their age. On the other hand, the youngest Hispanic respondents remain more likely than the non-Hispanic respondents their age to wear religious symbols and to have religious art or altars in their homes and are even somewhat more likely than Hispanic respondents who are slightly older (ages 30-35) to do so.

For the non-Hispanic respondents, membership in a Small Christian Community may serve to tie its participants more closely to their parish and, perhaps for the minority of young adults who are highly religious, to affirm and strengthen their religious identity in the face of its abandonment by the majority of their peers. The study's extended interviews with those who work with SCCs of young adults report that these Small Christian Communities tend to attract mostly conservative participants. The larger survey finds the same thing: respondents who are under thirty-five are significantly less likely than older respondents to cite "freedom from the institutional Church" as the best part of being a member of an SCC. Future studies should investigate whether Hispanic young adult Catholics are beginning to resemble their non-Hispanic age peers in becoming more tied to their parishes through Small Christian Community membership.

Gender Differences in Religious Participation

As was noted above, young adult Catholic women have become less observant in their attendance, less orthodox in their beliefs, and less likely to remain Catholic than young adult Catholic males, a reversal of the pattern of previous generations.[20] In the current study, there were no significant differences between men and women in their level of activity in SCCs, but there were other differences between the sexes in their religious practices:

• Women were more likely than men to report praying, especially during the pandemic.

• Women were more likely to report wearing religious symbols such as crucifixes and to participate in non-Mass religious celebrations.

• Women in SCCs were more likely than male members to cite spiritual reasons for their participation.

[20] See Davidson et al., *Search for Common Ground*, and D'Antonio, Dillon, and Gautier, *American Catholics in Transition*.

• There are more all-women SCCs than there are all-male or mixed-gender groups.

On the other hand, the women are also more likely than the men to report that they have struggled with their faith. Again, this may simply mean that their faith is important enough to take seriously, but the women respondents are also significantly more likely than the men to say that the allegations of Catholic clergy sexually abusing minors and its teachings on homosexuality and birth control bother them sufficiently that they have made them less likely to participate in parish life.

It would be interesting to know whether these gender differences are greater or less for Hispanic Catholics than for non-Hispanic Catholics and whether young adult Hispanic Catholics are becoming more like their non-Hispanic Catholic age peers in this regard. If older, first-generation Hispanic Catholic immigrant women are more religious along these dimensions than Hispanic Catholic men their age, is this also true for young adult Hispanic Catholic women? Or are young adult Hispanic Catholic women becoming more like their non-Hispanic peers in increasingly distancing themselves from the Church? The current study's data, unfortunately, were insufficient to answer these questions.

Concluding Reflections

While membership in a Small Christian Community is a key factor in connecting some Catholics with Catholicism in general and with their parish in particular, this appears to be true for only certain categories of Catholics. Particularly among non-Hispanic young adults, it is primarily the atypically conservative, evangelistic minority who participate in SCCs or are active in their parishes. Their SCCs tend to be centered around traditional prayer practices such as Eucharistic Adoration. Several of the interviewees who work with Small Christian Communities noted:

I see these major obstacles of women are second class and the gay-lesbian issue is very strong to discourage young people. So, you're getting a more conservative evangelical young person coming to church on Sunday. That's my experience.

If you're going to get young people involved, they want to do it hands-on. I don't think like if you just have a pure prayer group you'll attract a specific group like evangelical Catholics. Well, maybe go toward Eucharistic adoration, for example, or they'll go through saying the rosary. But the more progressive young people, I think it's the different activities, the outreach. . . . As I go around the United States, almost every young person says we have to do something about climate change. And they gave me a new word that I had not heard before: "climate justice."

As the second chapter noted, there is a need to reach out to more progressive young Catholics: "This may mean incorporating more discussion (and activities) focusing on social issues at the forefront of mainstream society (e.g., LBGTQ advocacy and support, climate justice, and racial justice). It may also mean exploring and addressing the discrepancy between the Church's teaching and mainstream practices among young adults, such as cohabiting before marriage." Chapter 7 makes a similar recommendation.

These observations have important implications for the future of Catholicism in this country. Since the non-Hispanic seminarians and the novices currently in religious institutes are likely to have been previously active in their local parishes and in SCCs, they will also be likely to be drawn from the atypically conservative/evangelical minority of non-Hispanic young adult Catholics who participate in such groups. Such seminarians, once ordained, may antagonize or alienate the congregations in parishes where they are stationed and may also deter many of their age peers from joining such parishes.

Hispanic SCCs appear to attract a differently-oriented population. While they are more likely to evangelize persons who want to grow in their faith, to practice charismatic prayer, to go on retreats, and to celebrate Mass together, they are also more likely to socialize with each other, to engage in service activities, and to collect donations for the needy. Again, to the extent that Hispanic seminarians and novices in religious institutes come from being active in these SCCs or in their local parishes, they will bring this spiritual focus with them. The differing theological and ecclesial perspectives of Hispanic seminarians/priests as compared to non-Hispanic seminarians/priests—or between Hispanic and non-Hispanic entrants to religious institutes—will need to be addressed and embraced by their formation programs. As Chapter 5 will point out, the Latino Pastoral Leaders Initiative (LPLI) has recommended the declericalization of Church leadership: "That is, effectively reaching beyond the 'usual suspects,' those regularly engaged with the parish and other vehicles of Church life, in order to reach those on the margins, which includes a growing number of youthful, disaffiliated Catholics as well as the searchers or seekers who have lost all interest in institutional religion."

Will seminaries and novitiates attempt to mold their Hispanic members into the more clerical non-Hispanic model, or will they allow new models to develop so that future priests and religious can reach out to those they are being trained to serve? This will be vitally important if the Church is to be able to welcome Hispanics in the future. Several interviewees said that, currently, Hispanics do not feel welcome in many parishes or feel culturally out of place. As Chapter 2 noted, Hispanic Small Christian Communities often have different ways of conducting their meetings and attract a wider variety of participants:

> [T]here's a great difference. The notion of fraternal communion, the notion of a lived experience and appreciating the real life, is much more profound in small communities with Hispanic Latinos.

*I find a lot more diversity in the Hispanic community, which
makes it for them very multicultural from the Hispanic point of
view.*

These differences may be off-putting when a person from one
ethnic culture considers joining a Small Christian Community
dominated by another cultural group.
Throughout its history, Catholicism has adapted to many
different cultures, both in its liturgy and in the daily living of
the faith. In the contemporary United States, the Church must
likewise speak to the different cultures of its members, not only
of different ethnic groups, but also of different generations and
of the intersections between ethnicity and generation. Additionally, cultural changes have occurred in the larger society,
especially in the changing roles and expectations of women in
the United States. To expect that all Catholic young adults or
Small Christian Communities will relate to a Church or a parish whose liturgies, religious education programs, and SCCs
are oriented to a single set of ethnic practices (e.g., of White
Anglophone Americans), a single (often older) generation, or
a single (usually male) gender is to present an unwelcoming
face to other religious seekers, whose gifts to Catholicism may
then be lost in this country.

CHAPTER FOUR

US Young Adult Catholics Discerning Spirituality and Family Life: What Is the Verdict?

Hosffman Ospino

Family is and has always been at the heart of conversations about Catholic spirituality as well as religious identity. It is in the context of the family that we learn the core values that are to guide us in life. In the family, we are expected to encounter the principles of our faith tradition, experience love, learn about relationships, and grow in the basic understandings that will shape our approach to reality. We form families usually mirroring the model of family life that we experienced growing up. The lack of a healthy family experience may certainly lead to the opposite of what any well-intentioned Christian may expect to find in the context of the family. Life is complex, and so is family life. If we want to understand how young adult Catholics in the United States live and practice their spirituality in connection to what happens in the family, we must factor into our considerations the hoped-for balance between the fragility and the greatness of our human condition, as individuals and as members of fluid social bodies.

In 2021, CARA published a report entitled *Faith and Spiritual Life of Catholics in the United States*.[1] The first and most robust

---

[1] Gray, Kramarek, and Gaunt, *Faith and Spiritual Life of Catholics.*

part of the report builds upon a national poll taking the pulse of how young adult Catholics in the country live out their spirituality. The second and third parts of the report explore the growing role of Small Christian Communities supporting Catholic spiritual life. In this chapter, I highlight key findings from the report while analyzing important realities that shape faith and spiritual life of US young adult Catholics in our day as they discern attitudes and commitments regarding family life.

What Family, What Spirituality?

When Catholics speak of family, we speak primarily of that essential social unit of mutual relationship in the context of a space called home. More specifically, family is "a community of persons: of husband and wife, of parents and children, of relatives."[2] A Catholic understanding of family is deeply rooted in the idea of life-giving mutuality among spouses, among parents and children, and among siblings. Anyone else invited into the sacredness of the home is welcomed into such mutuality and enriched by it. The family is a "domestic church,"[3] a place where people pray, practice charity and forgiveness, introduce one another to Jesus Christ and his message, and learn to care about themselves, others, and the created order.

The family reflects the intimacy of God as a community of divine persons: "The triune God is a communion of love, and the family is its living reflection."[4] Few images have been as influential as that of the Holy Family in shaping our Catholic

---

[2] Pope John Paul II, Apostolic Exhortation *Familiaris Consortium* (Rome: November 22, 1981), 18.

[3] See Second Vatican Council, Dogmatic Constitution on the Church, *Lumen Gentium* (November 21, 1964), 11.

[4] Pope Francis, Post-Synodal Apostolic Exhortation *Amoris Laetitia* (Rome: March 19, 2016), 11.

imagination when reflecting about life in the context of the home: "The covenant of love and fidelity lived by the Holy Family of Nazareth illuminates the principle which gives shape to every family, and enables it better to face the vicissitudes of life and history."[5]

Family is a vocation. For the baptized, such a particular vocation builds upon the universal call to holiness.[6] Catholics enter into the experience of forming families as disciples of Jesus Christ. Consequently, family life is a privileged opportunity to give witness to what we believe and who we are as Christians—first to those with whom we partake at home and, from there, to the larger church and society. Through marriage, and more specifically through the sacrament of matrimony, Catholic spouses actualize the call to holiness, affirm the sacredness of their mutual love, and receive each other by freely embracing a bond that is indissoluble.[7] The family is sustained by "a partnership of married life and love."[8] While much can be said about the inner workings of family life, Catholics, particularly since the Second Vatican Council, have paid increasing attention to how the family contributes to the construction of a better world. This requires that the Church as an institution dedicate appropriate resources to support families and the ministries that accompany them. Pope Francis reminds us that families are the "leaven of evangelization in society."[9] Echoing the conclusions from the 2014 Synod on the Family, the pope writes: "The family is thus an agent of pastoral activity through its explicit proclamation of the Gospel and its legacy of varied forms of witness, namely solidarity with the poor, openness to a diversity of people, the protection of creation, moral and

---

[5] Paul VI, *Address in Nazareth*, January 5, 1964, cited in *Amoris Laetitia*, 66.

[6] See *Lumen Gentium*, 40.

[7] See *Amoris Laetitia*, 61–66, 71–75.

[8] See Second Vatican Council, Pastoral Constitution on the Church in the Modern World, *Gaudium et Spes* (December 7, 1965), 48.

[9] *Amoris Laetitia*, 290.

material solidarity with other families, including those most in need, commitment to the promotion of the common good and the transformation of unjust social structures, beginning in the territory in which the family lives, through the practice of the corporal and spiritual works of mercy."[10]

This brief summary of key convictions about family life suggests that Catholic families hold a set of basic spiritual convictions that help them live their vocation in the everyday. One may argue that families rarely, if ever, engage in sophisticated theological reflections like the ones above to name their self-understanding. Also, one may object to the use of archetypes such as the Trinity or the Holy Family as models, especially when we are aware of the complex realities that challenge family life in our day. Nonetheless, we must start somewhere. We need reference points that help families aspire to a goal, even if utopian,[11] and assess themselves against criteria that transcend precisely their complex immediacy.

CARA's *Faith and Spiritual Life of Catholics in the United States* report does not focus explicitly on attitudes toward family life or marriage among young Catholics. Only a quarter (25%) of respondents to the 2020 National Poll on Young Catholics are married; 61 percent have never married. The report, nevertheless, provides glimpses of how the Catholic imagination remains rather strong in the basic understanding of family. Allow me to highlight three such glimpses. First, more than two-thirds of respondents (69%) to the poll shared that the Church's teachings about divorce and remarriage are not necessarily major deterrents—if they are, "only a little"—to be active in parish life.[12] Second, Catholics engaged in Small Christian Communities commented that prayer was important to improve their marriages and family life.[13] Third, young adult

---

[10] *Amoris Laetitia*, 290.
[11] Read *utopian* not as "impossible" but as "ideal and worth pursuing."
[12] Gray, Kramarek, and Gaunt, *Faith and Spiritual Life of Catholics*, 41.
[13] Gray, Kramarek, and Gaunt, 126.

Catholics—at least those participating in the poll and the surveys in the report—did not seem to have an activist stance about LGBTQ+ persons and family life. Only 10 percent of groups in the survey on Small Christian Communities say they reach out explicitly to this population.[14] As we will see, young adult Catholics' approach to the institutional Church's teachings on same-sex marriage may be evolving via a pragmatic approach—that is, by increasingly accepting social norms without directly confronting ecclesiastical authorities or doctrine. Furthermore, an interviewee commented that Small Christian Communities "tend to attract more conservative Catholics while young people overall tend to be more progressive. Thus, there is a need to reach out more to the progressive types . . . incorporating more discussion (and activities) focusing on social issues at the forefront of the mainstream society such as LBGTQ."[15]

While most participants in the studies underlying the report seem to hold strongly traditional Catholic convictions about family and marriage, these young adults Catholics do so in a fast-changing sociocultural landscape that often puts those convictions to the test—and manages to change them.

Negotiating Commitments to the Idea of Catholic Family Life in a Pluralistic Society

Anyone who has lived sixty to a hundred years in the United States has seen more changes in the way family life and marriage are defined—and redefined—than perhaps entire generations combined in any other society in previous centuries. The changes between 1920 and 2020 have been simply breathtaking. The following ten realities give us a sense of what has been happening:

---

[14] Gray, Kramarek, and Gaunt, 110.
[15] Gray, Kramarek, and Gaunt, 154.

1. In 1920, the marriage rate (i.e., number of marriages per year) in the US was 12 per 1,000 population (i.e., 1.2%); in 2019, it was 6.1 per 1,000 population (i.e., 0.61%).[16]

2. In 1920, the divorce rate (i.e., number of divorces per year) in the US was 12 per 1,000 population (i.e., 1.2%); in 2019, it was 2.7 per 1,000 population (i.e., 0.27%).[17] Although it seems that there are fewer divorces today, one must make note of sociologist Mark Gray's observation: "In aggregate terms, fewer marriages means fewer divorces."[18]

3. In 1920, the estimated median age at first marriage was 24.6 for men and 21.2 for women. By 2020, the median age at first marriage rose to 30.5 for men and 28.1 for women.[19]

4. In 1967, about 72 percent of people older than 18 in the US were married, 7.6 percent lived alone, and 0.4 percent lived with an unmarried partner. In 2021, about 50 percent of people older than 18 lived with a spouse, 15 percent lived alone, and 8 percent lived with an unmarried partner.[20]

---

[16] See data available in the US Centers for Disease Control and Prevention's National Vital Statistics System, https://www.cdc.gov/nchs/index.htm.

[17] See National Vital Statistics System. A starker contrast emerges when comparing the divorce rate between 1867 (0.3 per 1,000 population) and 1946 (4.3 per 1,000 population). The rate of divorces increased 6,000% in those seven decades. See Edward R. Callahan, "Divorce: A Survey," *The American Catholic Sociological Review* 9, no. 3 (October 1948): 164.

[18] Cited in Nate Madden, "Despite low Catholic marriage numbers, some see trend turning around," *National Catholic Reporter*, March 23, 2015, https://www.ncronline.org/news/parish/despite-low-catholic-marriage-numbers-some-see-trend-turning-around.

[19] See "Decennial Censuses, 1890 to 1940, and Current Population Survey, March and Annual Social and Economic Supplements, 1947 to 2021," from the US Census Bureau, available online at https://www.census.gov/data/tables/time-series/demo/families/marital.html.

[20] See "America's Families and Living Arrangements: 2021," a report from the US Census Bureau based on the Current Population Survey, 2021 Annual Social and Economic Supplement, November 29, 2021, https://www.census.gov/data/tables/2021/demo/families/cps-2021.html.

5. In 1920, about 21.4 percent of women participated in the labor force. In 2019, 59.4 percent did.[21]

6. About 3 percent of US women born between 1940 and 1944 lived in a cohabitating arrangement before the age of 25; so did 8 percent of men. These proportions increased to 37 percent (women) and 36 percent (men) in the same age range in the cohort of those born between 1960 and 1964.[22] According to the National Survey of Family Growth, between 2015 and 2019, 65 percent of women between the ages of 25 and 29 and 72 percent of women between ages 40 and 44 reported to have ever cohabitated.[23]

7. In 1960, 62 percent of young adults (ages 18-34) had their own households; most were married. The percentage of young adults in this same age range with their own households dropped to 32 percent in 2014.[24]

8. In 1960, 20 percent of young adults (ages 18-34) lived with their parents—a drastic decline from 35 percent in 1940. Most, however, were engaged in romantic relationships and forming families. In 1960, barely one in nine adults older than twenty-five had never been married. In 2014, 32 percent of young adults lived with parents or a parent, and the majority were not involved in any romantic relationship. Young adult men (35%) are more likely to live

---

[21] See 2020 data from "Women in the Labor Force: A Databook," an annual report from the US Bureau of Labor Statistics, https://www.bls.gov/cps/demographics.htm#women. In 2019, 69.2% of all men participated in the labor force.

[22] See Larry L. Bumpass and James A. Sweet, "National Estimates of Cohabitation," *Demography* 26, no. 4 (November 1989): 619.

[23] See Wendy D. Manning, Susan L. Brown, and Krista K. Payne, "Does Cohabitation Compensate for Marriage Decline?," *Contexts* 20, no. 2 (May 2021): 68–69.

[24] See Richard Fry, "For First Time in Modern Era, Living with Parents Edges Out Other Living Arrangements for 18- to 34-Year-Olds," *Pew Research Center*, May 24, 2016.

in this type of arrangement than young adult women (29%). Today, the percentage of young adults living with their parents and not involved in romantic relationships outpaces that of young adults married or living with a partner in their own household. Pew Research estimates that a quarter of adults in the United States may never marry.[25]

9. In 1958, Gallup reported that only 4 percent of the US population approved of interracial marriages, referring primarily to marriages between White and Black partners. At the time, interracial marriages were outlawed in more than 60 percent of the states in the nation. In 1967, the US Supreme Court ruled interracial marriages as legal. In 2021, Gallup reported that 94 percent of the US population approves of interracial marriages, with some minor resistance among people older than fifty (9% of this group still disapproves).[26] In 2019, about 11 percent of all adults in the country were married to a person of a different race or ethnicity. In that same year, Pew Research reported that "30% of Hispanic newlyweds married someone who is not Hispanic, a similar share to Asian newlyweds (29%) and a higher share than among Black (20%) and White (12%) newlyweds."[27] This is significantly relevant, mindful that about half of all Catholics in the country are Hispanic and that Asian Catholics are the fastest-growing group in the Church.

---

[25] See Fry, "For First Time in Modern Era."

[26] See Justin McCarthy, "U.S. Approval of Interracial Marriage at New High of 94%," *Gallup*, September 10, 2021, https://news.gallup.com/poll/354638/approval-interracial-marriage-new-high.aspx.

[27] See Mark Hugo Lopez, Jens Manuel Krogstad, and Jeffrey S. Passel, "Who Is Hispanic?," *Pew Research Center*, September 23, 2021, https://www.pewresearch.org/fact-tank/2021/09/23/who-is-hispanic/.

10. In 2000, the US Census Bureau reported that there were 594,000 same-sex, unmarried couples in the country.[28] That number increased to 901,997 same-sex couple households in 2010, with various spousal arrangements based on laws and recognitions at the state level.[29] In 2015, the US Supreme Court recognized the right of same-sex couples to marry. As of 2019, there were about 980,000 same-sex couple households in the country, 52 percent of whom were married and 48 percent of whom were cohabitating. Of the total 66,427,835 coupled households in the country in 2019, 1.5 percent were same-sex.

Just as breathtaking as these statistics are (and I am sure we can add a few more), these changes have also been swift. It took centuries for some European societies to codify marriage laws and for the Catholic Church to somewhat pair these to canon law. For centuries, Christian theologians, usually celibate clerics, limited themselves to comment on ideas about family and marriage deduced largely from reading religious texts.[30] All this changed dramatically in the twentieth century. Just as one generation in the United States was coping with the effects of women joining the workforce in large numbers, the next one was learning the effects of contraception and the striking drop in the number of children per family. The next

---

[28] See Tavia Simmons and Martin O'Connell, "Married-Couple and Unmarried-Partner Households: Census 2000 Special Reports," *US Census Bureau*, February 2003, https://www.census.gov/library/publications/2003/dec/censr-5.html.

[29] See Martin O'Connell and Sarah Feliz, "Same-sex Couple Household Statistics from the 2010 Census: SEHSD Working Paper Number 2011–26," *US Census Bureau: Social, Economic, and Housing Statistics Division*, September 27, 2011, https://www.census.gov/library/working-papers/2011/demo/SEHSD-WP2011-26.html.

[30] See, for instance, Philip Lyndon Reynolds, *How Marriage Became One of the Sacraments: The Sacramental Theology of Marriage from Its Medieval Origins to the Council of Trent* (New York: Cambridge University Press, 2016).

generation would have to face the precipitous decline—and
sometimes the deriding—of marriage as a social contract while
seeing cohabitation and divorce become a societal norm—for
some, an expectation. The very next generation, inheriting
changes that their parents and grandparents barely had time
to process, would come to terms with same-sex couples mar-
rying and forming families. Add to all this the large influx of
immigrants from various parts of the world; right now, about
13.7 percent of people living in the US are foreign-born. Not
only do they bring their own understandings about family life
and marriage as shaped by the cultures from which they come,
but they also have their own ways of and own struggles with
negotiating the fluid ideas about family life and marriage with
which they are confronted in our society.

In the meantime, core Catholic teachings about family and
marriage remain practically unchanged. Except for a more
contextualized analysis of family life encouraged by Vatican
II and a growing awareness of the fragility of family life (which
calls for intentional pastoral accompaniment), Catholic teaching in this area remains consistent across centuries—at least
since the Council of Trent. Some may see such consistency as
stubbornness. Others concede that we need to do more to
address the questions of our time. Pope Francis observes: "At
times we have also proposed a far too abstract and almost
artificial theological ideal of marriage, far removed from the
concrete situations and practical possibilities of real families.
This excessive idealization, especially when we have failed to
inspire trust in God's grace, has not helped to make marriage
more desirable and attractive, but quite the opposite."[31] Others
may see consistency, and even immutability, as a sign of faith-
fulness to tradition and the desire to hold onto firm founda-
tions. In the meantime, US Catholics have changed and will
likely continue to change as they find themselves negotiating

[31] *Amoris Laetitia*, 36.

the parameters defining Catholic identity, social belonging, citizenship, and gender roles, among others.

Let us look into five realities that allow us to assess, in rather broad terms, how US Catholics' practices and attitudes toward family life have been evolving in recent years:

1. *Matrimony (sacrament).* In 1970, the Catholic Church in the United States reported more than 425,000 sacramental marriages the previous year. At the time, the Catholic population in the country was about 54.1 million. By 2020, the Catholic population rose to about 74.4 million (34% increase), yet the number of registered sacramental marriages plummeted to slightly more than 131,000.[32]

2. *Divorce.* In 1948, the Jesuit sociologist Edward Callahan denounced divorce as "the national scandal in the United States."[33] The feeling evoked the sensibility of a religious community that at the turn of the twentieth century saw small rates of divorce or simply did not talk much about it, even though Catholics were not immune to realities such as family brokenness, separation, and desertion. Historically, Catholics have been less likely to divorce or separate compared to the rest of the US population. Good catechesis, active participation in sacramental life, and a positive perception of clerical authority seem to have contributed to this phenomenon. Nonetheless, the rate of divorce among Catholics today is closer to that of the general population than ever before.

A closer look at annulments (i.e., the declaration of a marriage as invalid or never having taken place) reveals an interesting picture. Between 1968 and 1978, the number of annulments in Catholic tribunals skyrocketed from 300 to 26,000. Most likely the reason was the streamlining

---

[32] See CARA, "Frequently Requested Church Statistics," http://cara.georgetown.edu/frequently-requested-church-statistics/.

[33] See Callahan, "Divorce: A Survey," 164.

of steps that made the process more available and wide-spread during this time.[34] The Canon Law Society in 1984 observed, however, that it was likely that the immense majority of potential petitioners of annulments, nine out of ten, did not seek the procedure. Annulments among Catholics peaked at 72,308 cases initiated in 1989. In 2019, 19,500 were initiated. To paraphrase Mark Gray's earlier observation, fewer Catholic marriages means fewer annulments.

In 2007, CARA reported that about 23% of adult Catholics had gone through a divorce; about half of them remarried or lived with a partner. Perhaps more telling, 76% of adult Catholics in the report believed divorce to be acceptable in "some cases" and 17% in "all cases." Half of Catholics saying that divorce was "not acceptable in any case" (7%) conceded exceptions such as physical abuse, emotional abuse and infidelity.[35]

3. *Cohabitation*. In 2007, about 4 percent of all adult Catholics were unmarried living with a partner. In 2015, that was the case for about 13 percent of Catholic parents ages 25 to 45.[36] While most Catholic couples are still married in the Church, in 2019, the Pew Research Center reported that 74 percent of Catholics considered cohabitation as acceptable.[37]

---

[34] See Dan Mintie, "Why Divorced Catholics Won't Just Go Away," in *U.S. Catholic* 49, no. 10 (October 1984): 6–12.

[35] See Mark M. Gray, Paul M. Perl, and Tricia C. Bruce, *Marriage in the Catholic Church: A Survey of U.S. Catholics* (Washington, DC: Center for Applied Research in the Apostolate, 2007).

[36] See Gray, Perl, and Bruce, *Marriage in the Catholic Church*, 18, and Mark M. Gray, *The U.S. Catholic Family: Demographics. The Second Special Report* (Washington, DC: Center for Applied Research in the Apostolate, 2015), 7.

[37] See Juliana Menasce Horowitz, Nikki Graf, and Gretchen Livingston, "Marriage and Cohabitation in the U.S.," *Pew Research Center*, November 6, 2019, https://www.pewresearch.org/social-trends/2019/11/06/marriage-and-cohabitation-in-the-u-s/.

4. *Children*. US Catholics born prior to 1942 were likely to have, on average, five or more children. In 2014, CARA reported that 5 percent of Catholic parents between ages 25 and 45 do not live with any children in their households, 29 percent live with one child, and 41 percent live with two children. About two-thirds (62%) of all adult Catholics do not live with a child in their household.[38] More than half (54%) of Catholic parents ages 25 to 45 are Hispanic.

5. *Attitudes toward same-sex relationships*. According to the Pew Research Center, attitudes toward same-sex marriage have practically reversed in the United States in less than two decades. In 2004, 60 percent of the US population opposed it while 31 percent expressed support. In 2019, 61 percent supported it, and 31 percent expressed opposition. During that same period of time, Catholics have followed a similar pattern. In 2004, 36 percent supported same-sex marriage. In 2019, 61 percent did.[39] In 2020, the American Values Survey, conducted by the Public Religion Research Institute, suggested that support for same-sex marriage could be as high as 70 percent among Catholics, with 78 percent in support among those of Hispanic background.[40]

Lastly, any reflection on how young adult Catholics in the United States discern the relationship between spirituality and family life requires paying close attention to key realities that

[38] See Gray, *U.S. Catholic Family*, 6.

[39] See data from the Pew Research Center's Fact Sheet, "Attitudes on Same-Sex Marriage," May 14, 2019, https://www.pewforum.org/fact-sheet/changing-attitudes-on-gay-marriage/.

[40] See "Amid Multiple Crises, Trump and Biden Supporters See Different Realities and Futures for the Nation," *Public Religion Research Institute*, October 19, 2020, https://www.prri.org/research/amid-multiple-crises-trump-and-biden-supporters-see-different-realities-and-futures-for-the-nation/.

affect Hispanics, who constitute nearly 45 percent of the
Catholic body in this country. In general, Hispanics are a very
young population, with a median age of twenty-nine. As of
2017, about 50.5 percent of US Catholics between eighteen and
forty-nine were Hispanic.[41] To speak of young adult ministry
in many parts of the country means accompanying Hispanic
Catholics. Among the main challenges that affect Hispanic
young adult Catholics today, we can name high poverty rates;
low educational attainment, especially at the higher education
level; and immigration-related challenges, especially for the
millions whose migratory status is irregular. All these have a
serious impact upon how Hispanics form families and estab-
lish priorities regarding their spiritual lives.[42]

Who Are Young Adult Catholics Listening to on Matters of Family Life?

From an institutional perspective and in an ideal world, the
expectation is that all Catholics would listen to Church leaders
and established teachings on matters related to marriage and
family life. With that perspective, we would also assume that
Church teachings on these areas are crystal clear to all in the
fold. However, we must come to terms with the fact that US
young adult Catholics are constantly negotiating their identity
in a changing society in which Catholic values regularly com-
pete in the marketplace of pluralistic ideas. While this population seems to be aware of basic Catholic teachings about
family life (influenced by catechesis, cultural practice, or

---

[41] Estimates emerging from demographic data analysis developed for the
2018 Fifth National Encuentro of Hispanic Ministry, convoked by the United
States Conference of Catholic Bishops.

[42] See Hosffman Ospino, "Hispanics and Family Life in Twenty-First
Century America: A Catholic Call to Action," in *Renewing Catholic Family Life
and Spirituality: Experts Explore New Directions in Family Spirituality and Family
Ministry*, ed. Gregory K. Popcak (Huntington, IN: Our Sunday Visitor, 2020),
299–312.

simply the sway of Catholic upbringing), as we saw above, they seem to mirror behaviors and attitudes more consistent with those of the wider population.

If one were to name the most influential sources of opinion—and, quite likely, value formation—for today's young adults, Catholic and non-Catholic, social media rises to the top. Research has demonstrated that social networking sites promote and effectively encourage religious syncretism among emerging Catholics.[43] The influence of social networking sites and on-demand television, among other forms of individualized media venues geared not only to entertain but also to shape public opinion and cajole preconceived praxis (e.g., purchasing something to support a particular individual or cause), remains understudied in the Catholic world. Attitudes and perspectives about marriage and family life are constantly being defined by social media. Ironically, many—most?—Catholic pastoral leaders seem to be oblivious about using social media to engage their constituencies, especially the young. Respondents to the National Poll of Young Adult Catholics reported that, in 2020, amidst the COVID-19 pandemic that practically brought the nation to a halt, only 18 percent of young adults were contacted by their parishes, most of them because they were registered, and just a fraction were contacted via social media.[44] We may read this as a missed opportunity but also an urgent call to do better in accompanying young adults and their families through times of crisis using social media.

But social networking sites do not and should not have the last word in shaping attitudes and convictions about marriage and family life. The *Faith and Spiritual Life of Catholics in the United States* report highlights important trends for Church

---

[43] See Paul K. McClure, "Faith and Facebook in a Pluralistic Age: The Effects of Social Networking Sites on the Religious Beliefs of Emerging Adults," *Sociological Perspectives* 59, no. 4 (2016): 818–34.

[44] See Gray, Kramarek, and Gaunt, *Faith and Spiritual Life of Catholics*, 72.

leaders and educators to imagine strategies and commitments to more intentionally engage young adult Catholics—and others—on questions in these important areas of spiritual and social identity.

CARA estimates that, in 2018, there were 20,621,578 young adult Catholics between the ages of eighteen and thirty-five living in the country.[45] By and large, young adults Catholics hold on to their faith and religious identity. Seven in ten have received the sacraments of initiation, and nine in ten are cradle Catholics.[46] Although not all are highly involved in religious activities, they still call themselves Catholics.

The report confirms that parishes are far from being the center of spiritual life for the majority of young adult Catholics: "Prior to the pandemic, 13% of Catholic young adults attended Mass at least once a week. Twenty-one percent attended Mass less than weekly, but at least once a month. Thirty-one percent attended Mass a few times a year. Thirty-six percent say they rarely or never attend Mass."[47] Mass attendance has further declined during the pandemic and may not see a strong increase in the near future.[48] Chapter 1 offers an analysis of young adult Catholic involvement with their faith within and beyond parish life. Besides attending Mass regularly or sporadically, about 64 percent of young adult Catholics are not involved *at all* in parish ministries and activities.[49] This reality suggests that the majority of this population may not necessarily be drawing their spiritual sustenance or informing their opinions about marriage and family life from their priests or through formal catechesis.

Although much of the Church's pastoral activity to support family life happens in parishes, what young adult Catholics

---

[45] Gray, Kramarek, and Gaunt, 25.
[46] Gray, Kramarek, and Gaunt, 22.
[47] Gray, Kramarek, and Gaunt, 37.
[48] Gray, Kramarek, and Gaunt, 70.
[49] Gray, Kramarek, and Gaunt, 40.

are hearing and seeing in some parishes may be producing the opposite effect. The following analysis from the report is very telling:

> Forty-four percent of respondents said that allegations of clergy sexually abusing minors has made them less likely to be active in parish life "somewhat" or "very" much. Forty-two percent say the Church's teachings on homosexuality similarly make them less likely to be active in parish life. Next, a feeling that older generations have too much influence in their parish make 35% "somewhat" or "very" much less likely to be active in parish life. Other factors with a similar influence are the Church's teachings on birth control (34% "somewhat" or "very" much less likely), the roles available to women in the Church (33%), a feeling that the Church is not open to dialog with other religious faiths (33%), and the Church's teachings on divorce and remarriage (32%).[50]

The steady distancing from regular parish life, however, stimulated by a perceived sense of hypocrisy and inauthenticity in various sectors of the Church, does not mean that young adult Catholics have given up on the communal character of their faith—or the parish altogether. In other words, this population longs for community. While most may not see themselves as members of community in the larger context of the parish, they seem to do so in small ecclesial communities or groups. Most of these groups (66%) are meeting at parishes.[51] About 58 percent of young adult Catholics report to be involved in a small faith group, mainly Bible study communities.[52] Looking closely at data from the 2020 National Survey of Small Christian Communities, it is interesting to observe that participating groups report about five to six young adults

---

[50] Gray, Kramarek, and Gaunt, 41.
[51] Gray, Kramarek, and Gaunt, 102.
[52] Gray, Kramarek, and Gaunt, 36.

(ages 18-34) on average attending a typical meeting.[53] Most members participating in these groups are married with children;[54] most are women.[55]

The spiritual benefits of participating in small ecclesial communities on the lives of those participating seem to be manifold. This seems to be a major area of possibilities for pastoral planning for pastoral leaders and organizations. About 19 percent of people engaged in these ecclesial communities and 42 percent of respondents in mainly Hispanic groups feel that participation has "improved marriage and family life."[56] Among those who completed the National Survey of Small Christian Communities, 84 percent acknowledge that participation fosters community and friendship; 82 percent see the benefits of sharing and exchanging. For 76 percent of respondents, personal or spiritual growth is a major benefit, and 62 percent feel that the best part of being a member is prayer, praise, and worship.[57] For Hispanic immigrants in particular, as suggested in Chapter 3, membership in small ecclesial communities "[helps] them and their families preserve important elements of the faith from their homelands in the face of a strange and overpowering American culture." One can only anticipate the effects of such benefits upon participants' spiritual development and the strengthening of family life.

The Verdict?

On the question of how US young adult Catholics negotiate their Catholic identity and spirituality, particularly on matters related to marriage and family life, my sense is that the jury is

[53] Gray, Kramarek, and Gaunt, 115.
[54] Gray, Kramarek, and Gaunt, 113.
[55] Gray, Kramarek, and Gaunt, 116.
[56] Gray, Kramarek, and Gaunt, 126.
[57] Gray, Kramarek, and Gaunt, 125–26.

still out. The ecclesial institution and its authorities continue to lose ground steadily in terms of influencing the lives of young adult Catholics as they make decisions about relationships, household arrangements, sexual activity, marriage, perceptions about same-sex relationships, and even parenting. If the parish was ever a source of formation and communal life that couples and families sought for support, this does not seem to be the case today. Most young adult Catholics do not seem to resonate with what happens regularly in parishes. Such a reality demands that Catholic pastoral leaders and educators ask constantly, "Where does ministry to young adults need to be taking place?" (see Chapter 7). Catholic perceptions about marriage, children, and family seem to be channeled through the extreme lens of ideological polarization, as suggested by sociologist of religion Mary Ellen Konieczny,[58] rather than through dialogue committed to fostering faithful communion and mutual understanding.

Yet, there are signs of hope that should serve as sources of encouragement for the entire Catholic community. Not all young adult Catholics have given up on their faith, their Church, and the desire to cultivate their spiritual life. We have more than 20.6 million Catholics ages eighteen to thirty-five to accompany and support. They seem to be eager for their institution, pastoral leaders, educators, and theologians to put forth our best resources in helping them negotiate the fast-changing realities about marriage and family life with which they are confronted every day. We need a renewed commitment to adult catechesis, without a doubt. Yet, repeating established doctrines as unchanging or as the only alternatives to the complexity and mysterious dimensions of human experience may not be enough. We must take seriously the real lives of individuals, couples, and families in the here and now

---

[58] See Mary Ellen Konieczny, *The Spirit's Tether: Family, Work, and Religion among American Catholics* (New York: Oxford University Press, 2013).

of history, exploring ways to affirm and embrace instead of excluding and condemning. Small faith communities are nurturing the lives of young adult Catholics. In them, these Catholics listen to one another, pray, and learn how to sustain their spirituality as well as their families. However, they need to listen to other voices, and such other voices cannot be only those coming from social media or the polarizing forces that undermine communion. Hispanic Catholics, both immigrant- and US-born, draw from rich cultural and religious traditions of profound communal character and bring a renewed passion for family life that often stands as countercultural to predominant individualistic social mores. We can say something similar of the many Asian, Black, and Native American Catholics transforming faith communities everywhere.

In the midst of these circumstances, the jury is out and may well result in a hung jury. This means that Catholics will have to learn to trust one another in the Spirit, repeatedly reread the tradition theologically and pastorally with fresher eyes and open minds, and accept the responsibility to take seriously the questions that shape the religious and social imaginations of young adult Catholics in our day.

CHAPTER FIVE

New Pastoral-Theological Directions on the Faith, Spirituality, and Leadership Formation of Hispanic/Latinx Youth and Young Adults in Light of CARA's Research

Allan Figueroa Deck, SJ

CARA presented the preliminary results of a major study, titled "Faith and Spiritual Life of Catholics in the United States" in February 2021. The study elicited a significant amount of Hispanic/Latinx youth and young adult participation and consisted of (1) a national poll of young adult Catholics, (2) a national survey of Small Christian Communities, and (3) interviews about the Small Christian Community (SCC) experience. The survey, which included 2,214 youth and young adult subjects between the ages of eighteen and thirty-five, was conducted in the first few months of the COVID-19 pandemic. Consequently, it was able to capture basic features of the communities' responses to what some are calling a watershed moment in the evolution of Church practices into the future.

The strong Hispanic/Latinx participation in the survey and interviews is notable; it accounted for 43 percent of the respondents, while non-Hispanic Whites accounted for 44 percent. There are many reasons to concur with the observation that

Hispanic/Latinx youth and young adults are indeed leading indicators of the present and future reality of US Catholicism, as well as that of other faiths, for demographic reasons if no other.[1] In this chapter, I will center on some possible new directions for the emerging status of Hispanic/Latinx leadership within the larger matrix of US Catholicism. In doing so, I aim to highlight the findings regarding household or domestic religious practice, which represents the area of greatest divergence between the Hispanic/Latinx survey participants and the non-Hispanic/Latinx participants. I will also reflect upon neuralgic concerns that arose among the Hispanic/Latinx interviewees. These concerns highlight the urgent need to develop new paradigms for leadership that flow from Pope Francis's call for *missionary option* and *pastoral conversion*. Before addressing these topics, however, a brief overview of the poll findings and the survey of SCCs will help contextualize and shed light on concerns raised in the interviews.

Findings

The findings of this major study are quite extensive and include data on the salient characteristics of the young adult faithful of all racial/ethnic backgrounds: demographics, schooling, marital status, regional distribution, and level of engagement with their Catholic faith through the reception of the sacraments, Mass attendance, spiritual practices, participation in religious education, and Catholic schools. The survey and interviews shed significant light on several aspects of the reality: parish life, Catholic communities, movements and

[1] Social science researchers Putnam and Campbell were among the first to use the term "leading indicators" with reference to Hispanics/Latinx in their memorandum to the United States Conference of Catholic Bishops (USCCB). See Robert D. Putnam and David E. Campbell, "The Changing Face of American Catholicism: A Memo" (Washington, DC, May 22, 2008).

groups, faith at home and in everyday life, and the effects of the pandemic.

The survey spotlights the current state of affairs, particularly with respect to parish life and to SCCs and movements, which function both within and outside the parish structure. First, let us look at parish participation as reflected in attendance at Mass and related activities.

Regarding Parish-Based Activities

- Before the pandemic, just 13 percent of Catholic young adults attended Mass at least once a week. Twenty-one percent attend less than weekly, but at least once a month. Thirty-one percent say they attend a few times a year. Thirty-six percent say they never attend Mass. Various reasons are given for not attending Mass once a week. The most common reason is not having time—57 percent. But close to that, at 55 percent, is not believing that Sunday Mass attendance binds one under condition of sin. Other reasons given by 43 percent of the respondents are that they are not very religious and/or *prefer practicing their faith outside the parish*. Unquestionably, this data confirms the widespread realization that youth and young adult Catholics are moving away from what is considered "normal" engagement with the institutional Catholic Church.

- Only 6 percent of respondents say they are very involved with parish activities and ministries beyond attending Mass. Thirteen percent say they are "somewhat" involved. Another 17 percent say they are a "little" involved. *Sixty-four percent say they are not at all involved*.

- A considerable number of respondents, 44 percent, say that the allegations of sexual abuse of minors have led them to be less active in parish life. Closely following that concern is another expressed by 42 percent of the respondents regarding their disagreement and discomfort with the Church's teaching on homosexuality. Thirty-five percent said the excessive influence of an older generation discouraged them from more involvement with their parish. Similarly, 34 percent voiced disagreement with the Church's teachings on contraception. Respondents also expressed difficulty in several other areas: 32 percent regarding the limitations of roles available to women in the Church, 33 percent regarding the perceived lack of willingness to dialogue with other religions, and 32 percent regarding the Church's teachings on divorce and remarriage.

• Finally, there are other parish-based activities that deserve mention, such as Eucharistic Adoration, in which 16 percent of respondents participate. Merely 17 percent participate in the sacrament of reconciliation once a year, 31 percent less than once a year, and 38 percent never.

Regarding Small Christian Communities (SCCs)

With regard to the participation of young adults in Catholic communities, movements, and church groups, these were some important findings:

• Only 15 percent of young adults say they are involved in a diocesan or parish group, while 20 percent have participated in volunteer groups sponsored by either religious institutes, the Knights of Columbus, pro-life groups, or the St. Vincent de Paul Society. Currently, then, it appears that organizations other than parishes and dioceses are slightly more engaged in young adult outreach. The overwhelming majority of youth, however, are disconnected from small groups.

• Thirty-four percent of the young adults participating in these groups indicated a regular involvement with a

Catholic community or group. The larger percentage of these communities or groups devote themselves to service and assistance to others and/or describe their work as evangelization, defined as spreading the faith to others.

• The main reasons the respondents give for participating in these small groups/communities is (1) to reduce negative feelings in themselves, (2) to nourish their spiritual life, and (3) to satisfy the need to learn from new experiences, to act upon one's convictions about serving others, and to strengthen social ties.

• Activities with young adults take place much more outside of the parish in schools, colleges and universities, some other public space, member's homes, or online. Forty-one percent take place in the parish.

Regarding Faith at Home and in Everyday Life

One of the more useful contributions of CARA's survey is the extent to which it identified domestic forms of religious practice. Scholarly work and discussions about religion in the United States have often taken a somewhat narrow *official practices approach* that highlights Sunday Mass attendance and reception of the sacraments in the urban and suburban middle-class context of the United States. Particularly in the case of Latinos, such an emphasis betrays a lack of understanding about the roots and nature of Latino Catholicism in the unique evangelization of Latin America five hundred years ago as well as current features of its significantly immigrant and working-class milieu. Latino Catholicism has deep medieval roots that antedate the standardizing and reform efforts of the Council of Trent.[2] CARA's survey correctly reflects this insight into the

[2] See Orlando O. Espín, "Popular Catholicism" and "Popular Religions," in *An Introductory Dictionary of Theology and Religious Studies*, ed. Orlando O. Espín and James B. Nickoloff (Collegeville, MN: Liturgical Press, 2007), 1058–60.

broader and somewhat anomalous character of popular religious forms and takes a more balanced and comprehensive approach by identifying a range of religious practices in the Latino context, thus paying more attention to household or domestic religion.[3] Theologian Orlando Espín and others have called attention to the fundamentally medieval and indigenous (Native American) spirit of Latin American Catholicism with its emphasis on mediations of images, saints, and home practices together with the relative dearth of clerical ministers on the one hand and an enthusiastic conflation of official religious and cultural celebrations on the other. Pope Francis has perceptively noted that, despite its insufficiencies and limits, the evangelization of Latin America five centuries ago was an outstanding success insofar as "the faith truly did become culture." It was Pope St. Paul VI in *Evangelii Nuntiandi* who asserted that true evangelization is not real until "faith becomes culture."[4] Pope Francis gives great importance to how in the Latin American experience of faith (and the experiences of others) becomes culture when, in *Evangelii Gaudium*, he maintains that popular piety is a significant source of evangelizing power: ". . . different peoples among whom the Gospel has been inculturated are *active, collective subjects or agents of evangelization.* This is so because each people is the creator of their own culture and the protagonist of their own history. . . .

---

[3] See Thomas Albert Howard, "Enough Bromides," *Commonweal* 148, no. 5 (May 2021): 34–37. In the context of interfaith dialogue, Howard explains the way elitism and Western categorization eschew popular, traditional expressions of belief and thus fail to capture the fuller reality of world religion. Something similar occurs, in my thinking, *mutatis mutandis* with the approach taken to popular religious expressions in polling and surveys. See also Howard's *The Faith of Others: A History of Interreligious Dialogue* (New Haven, CT: Yale University Press, 2021).

[4] Pope Paul VI, Apostolic Exhortation *Evangelii Nuntiandi* (Rome: December 8, 1975), 20.

Once the Gospel has been inculturated in a people, in the process of transmitting their culture they also transmit the faith in ever new forms; hence of the importance of understanding evangelization as inculturation."[5] Pope Francis goes on to say, citing the *Puebla Document*, that, ". . . a people continuously evangelize itself. Herein lies the importance of popular piety, a true expression of the spontaneous missionary activity of the people of God. This is an 'ongoing and developing process, *of which the Holy Spirit is the principal agent*' [emphasis added]."[6]

The clergy during Catholicism's long gestation in Latin America and the Caribbean were concentrated in a few cities, while the vast majority of people lived in isolated rural environments. Latin America never had anything near an adequate number of priests, vowed religious, or catechists to attend to a huge population of natives, African slaves, and soon-to-be mestizo and mulatto people. This situation inevitably resulted in a serious reduction of opportunities for the faithful to attend Mass or receive other sacraments such as reconciliation; hence, the Argentine theologian Rafael Tello made the fascinating observation that the evangelization of Latin America was effectively accomplished within the context of popular culture, not ecclesiastical culture. The parish system was relatively weak or even nonexistent; the clergy were only occasionally present.

This situation contrasts markedly with the influence of what can be called the "ecclesiastical bubble" of official Catholicism. Adherence to a parish in the way it historically occurred in the United States was hardly the practice in Latin America for centuries and even today, where people identify with chapels

---

[5] Pope Francis, *Evangelii Gaudium* (Rome: November 24, 2013), 122; emphasis added.

[6] See *Evangelii Gaudium*, 122; Third General Conference of Latin America and Caribbean Bishops, *Puebla Document* (Puebla, Mexico: 1979), 450; and Fifth General Conference of the Latin American and Caribbean Bishops, *Aparecida Document* (Aparecida, Brazil: 2007), 264.

devoted to their patron saint, confraternity churches, and vast mission stations of religious orders with little or no regard for the juridical parish. Popular Catholicism, as it is called, is primarily domestic and tends to pay more attention to family household practices and to cultural and civic observances imbued with religious significance than to obligations like attendance at Mass, going to confession, or being active parishioners, as such practices are infrequent and often not feasible.[7]

Anecdotally, and now in surveys including CARA's under discussion here, one learns how the pandemic experience beginning in 2020 has impacted religious practice. In the case of Latinos, however, something pertinent to the pandemic experience can be observed—namely that, among them, there exists a strong religious back-up and at least a partial alternative to the standardized practices such as Sunday Mass attendance. Under pandemic conditions, household religion centered around devotions, especially to the Virgin Mary under various titles such as Guadalupe, has flourished. The CARA survey tried to capture some of this reality with some success. The list is considerable: the recitation of the rosary, the use of holy water, home altars, Lenten fasting and abstinence, and the abundance of religious images of Christ, the Virgin Mary, and other saints. Moreover, there are seasonal gatherings, such as Christmas *posadas*, at people's homes, and small, home-based Christian community gatherings among sizable numbers of Latino Catholics. Both before and now, as the pandemic subsides, it appears that popular domestic religion has helped fill a void for Latinx communities who, in the survey, reported *significantly higher* participation than non-

---

[7] Argentine theologian Rafael Tello describes what he calls *pastoral popular*, popular pastoral ministry, as it evolved in Latin America over the past five hundred years. See Enrique Ciro Bianchi, *Pobres en este mundo, ricos en la fe* (Buenos Aires: Libros Agape, 2012), 11, and Allan Figueroa Deck, *Francis, Bishop of Rome: The Gospel for the Third Millennium* (New York: Paulist Press, 2016), 44–59.

Latinx in a range of home-centered or small community activities.

Another aspect of Hispanic/Latinx domestic religion is its *everydayness* or quotidian character. Theologian Carmen Nanko-Fernández raises up *lo cotidiano* as a fundamental characteristic of Hispanic/Latinx religion. She even defines it as a *locus theologicus* for the Hispanic/Latinx people: ". . . ordinary living is privileged as source, provides content, particularizes context, and marks the spaces and places from which Latinas do theology. Such theologizing avoids abstraction and is admittedly polyvocal and fluid."[8]

CARA's survey thus provides more substance to the notion that domestic religion, an expression of popular religion, is alive and well, given the relatively high percentages of Hispanic/Latinx who indicated their practice of many of its features. These practices have remained strong even, or especially, in the conditions of the pandemic.

Concerns of Those Interviewed Regarding SCCs and Other Matters

The interviewees for CARA's survey raised a number of concerns that correlate with the underlying challenges faced by the institutional Church in reaching out to youth, including Hispanic/Latinx young adults, during and after the COVID-19 pandemic. Naming these concerns is helpful in arriving at a qualitative analysis of the *Faith and Spiritual Life Survey* and engaging in further reflection regarding the meaning and consequences of the concerns that arise with the findings themselves. Here are some of the concerns that arose in the interviews:

---

[8] Carmen Nanko-Fernández, "Lo Cotidiano as Locus Theologicus," in *The Wiley Blackwell Companion to Latino/a Theology*, ed. Orlando O. Espín (Chichester, West Sussex: Wiley Blackwell, 2015), 15.

- A decrease in the number of accessible SCCs is a disincentive for church engagement among youth and young adults. The most basic services were financially supported by parishes and dioceses, but there has been a decline in budgets and paid positions for youth and young adult ministers, hence a serious understaffing problem for reaching out.

- There is a perception that pastors are uncommitted and unenthusiastic in supporting the creation and maintenance of SCCs.

- While large-scale youth events like World Youth Day and large convocations of associations like FOCUS or NCYC can attract many youth, they can also drain resources, time, and energy in fostering long-range infrastructure in youth and young adult ministry.

- There is a perceived general reluctance to actually *listen* to youth and young adults and grant them true *agency* in the ecclesial community. Youth leadership must be identified and valued not only in limited youth work but in the wider ecclesial community.

- The Church continues to suffer from an aura of hypocrisy and inauthenticity regarding its handling of issues of sexual abuse and racism, exacerbated by a tendency toward judgmentalism and exclusion.

- There is a need for differentiated approaches to youth and young adult ministries based on the diversity of factors, cultures, languages, etc. that characterize the Church. A one-size-fits-all approach will not do. SCCs sensitive to diversity are useful vehicles for gathering and ministering to youth, but they are not being fostered.

- It was opined that SCCs tend to attract conservative or more traditionally inclined young Catholics but not the more progressive ones, which suggests the need to address issues important to these particular youth such as anti-racism, climate justice, and LGBTQ issues. The impression given is that the Church is not opting for the alienated, socially active young people but catering to the demographically smaller, traditionally-oriented youth.

• While several interviews indicated that the local ecclesial community is increasingly aware of and responsive to social justice issues like racism and climate change, others voiced concerns that the action orientation of the SCCs is too limited to *ad intra* ecclesial concerns, to pro-life efforts, and to direct charity to the poor (for example, food distribution), rather than to a seamless garment of social morality and coherent advocacy for other justice issues and empowerment of the marginalized. These concerns are important and attractive to the most youthful generations.

Pastoral-Theological Reflections

The findings of the CARA survey and the views expressed by the interviewees provide rich soil for theological reflection, particularly of an ecclesiological nature. This reflection is particularly pertinent to the Hispanic/Latinx demographic which, as was seen, represents almost half the youthful population that participated in the survey and constitutes *de facto* the majority of young Catholics in the United States today.

The Retrieval and Resilience of Domestic Popular Religion

The vitality of popular Catholicism among the Hispanic/Latinx youth is seen in their responses to the questions about the prevalence of household or domestic religious practices, especially during the COVID-19 experience. This popular Catholicism obviously does not give the same importance to official Church practices, such as the Sunday Eucharist and reception of the sacraments, as Church authorities do, yet it remains a way in which the institutional Church exercises a soft power over the people. The pandemic is bringing to our attention the community's ability to find at least some viable outlets to continue the exercise of its faith in terms of everyday connections with God at home—*lo cotidiano*—that are dependent on family rather than on the parish or official clerical presence of priest, deacon, or consecrated religious. The pandemic highlights the persistence of household religion and may even result in a strengthening of it out of sheer necessity, not unlike the situation that prevailed centuries ago in rural Latin America, the historic homeland of today's Hispanic/ Latinx communities, at the origins of Catholicism's presence there.

Underneath the persistence of this domestic religion is a concept of church which privileges baptism over ministerial ordination because it revolves around the baptized themselves in their identity as a priestly people—the common priesthood. While this domestic faith has tended to be viewed as woefully inadequate for a robust, committed Catholic life today in the post-Christian, secular cultural environment of the United States, the pandemic has been an occasion for the ongoing significance of popular Catholicism to arise again and be valued as an expression of a truly resilient, inculturated faith, one that is lived and led by the non-ordained.

Popular Catholicism centered in the home consequently *reconfigures* ministry in the Church by stressing the agency of family—of the baptized laity—rather than that of the ordained. The ecclesial community exists and is structured more on the provision of *service and care* flowing from *baptism* than on the exercise of *juridical powers* flowing from *ordination*. This reconfiguration of Church is at least implicit, if not explicit, in the thinking of Pope Francis. It is key, for example, in his understanding of synodality. The emphasis he gives to baptism is reflected in the pope's use of the phrase "missionary disciples" as the most appropriate umbrella term to refer to the *one Christian vocation* all have received in baptism. In this, Pope Francis follows the lead of the *Aparecida Document*, which was among the first magisterial sources to repeatedly insist on using this category rather than the traditional references to "laity" and "clergy."[9]

Viewed in this way, the reality of domestic religion becomes an inadequate but nonetheless significant practice and resource for a Church seeking to *reconfigure* leadership effectively by placing that leadership, if only on a limited basis, in the hands of the laity. The prevalence of popular religion in its most fully developed expressions creates an environment that *re-centers* the life of the faith community in immediate family, extended family, and small groups, as well as simultaneously in the broader secular milieu, rather than in the official "ecclesiastical bubble." Looking at popular religion in this more generous and constructive way may offer the Church a new paradigm for inculturating the faith in today's fiercely secularizing environment. Moreover, the data are showing that the endurance of home-based and small community popular religious practices provide the faith with a presence in the secular environments of home, work, and social/civic settings proper to diverse cultural groups like the Hispanic/Latinx. It may be noted as well that the pandemic created opportunities for home or SCC-centered prayer and worship outside the official church structure through virtual gatherings perfectly capable of reaching out beyond the territorial limits of diocese and parish.

Toward the Reconfiguration of Ecclesial Leadership

A second reflection that emerges from the realization of the major role of Hispanic/Latinx youth and young adults in the shaping of today's and tomorrow's US Catholicism is the

---

[9] Fifth General Conference of the Bishops of Latin America and the Caribbean, *Aparecida Document*, 1.

challenge of reconfiguring the exercise of leadership in the Church. The Roundtable for Church Management recently began a leadership development program, the Latino Pastoral Leaders Initiative (LPLI), targeting both clergy and laity. The key elements of leadership identified by the Initiative constitute a creative response to the need for new attitudes and practices in line with the dramatic circumstances and change in demographics, socioeconomic concerns, interests, and attitudes of today's youth and young adults as demonstrated in the CARA survey findings and interviews. Moreover, the proposed elements of a reconfigured leadership flow very well from Pope Francis's urgent call for *pastoral conversion* and the assumption of a *missionary option* proposed in his *magna carta, Evangelii Gaudium.* The pope is calling for nothing less than a top-down and bottom-up revision of how the Church operates.[10] The pope describes this transformation in these incisive words: "I dream of a missionary option, that is, a missionary impulse capable of transforming everything, so that the Church's customs, ways of doing things, times and schedules, language and structures can be suitably channeled for evangelization of today's world rather than self-preservation. . . . The renewal of structures demanded by pastoral conversion can only be understood . . . as part of an effort to make them more mission-oriented, . . . more inclusive and open."[11]

The LPLI has identified these key elements of and for leadership development that assume the "missionary option" urged by Pope Francis and reflect the reality and concerns of youth and young adults in general but certainly the Hispanic/Latinx in particular, as revealed in the CARA interviews:

• De-clericalization of leadership

• Ongoing pastoral conversion

• Servant and synodal leadership

---

[10] Pope Francis, *Evangelii Gaudium*, 27.
[11] *Evangelii Gaudium*, 27.

- Leadership with Hispanic/Latinx presence and flair
- Leadership of reconciliation, justice, and peace
- New vision for Hispanic/Latinx leadership

In responding to the challenges faced by the Church as discovered in the recent CARA survey, the leadership program proposed by the Leadership Roundtable is very timely. The limits of this chapter do not allow us to go into great detail regarding each aspect of leadership furthered by the LPLI in its formation program. What follows here, nevertheless, is a brief description of each of the components of a reconfigured ministerial leadership for the Church today, one that corelates with the concerns expressed in the CARA interviews.[12]

1. ***De-clericalization*** is urgently needed in order to open the Church's life and practice to "going out," that is, effectively reaching beyond the "usual suspects"—those regularly engaged with the parish and other vehicles of Church life—in order to reach those on the margins, which includes a growing number of youthful, disaffiliated Catholics as well as the searchers or seekers who have lost all interest in institutional religion. The limited number of priests and consecrated religious is woefully inadequate for a Church that claims to be reaching out and missionary. The inadequacy of the Church's ministerial organization is due in large measure to a lack of pastoral agents. With its narrow configuration of ministry, clericalism excessively limits the scope of activity open to missionary disciples and constrains their participation in several ways.[13]

---

[12] See Latino Pastoral Leaders Initiative of the Leadership Roundtable, "What We Do," https://leadershiproundtable.org/what-we-do/lpli.

[13] Allan Figueroa Deck, "Clericalism: Neuralgic Point of Church Reform," in *Pope Francis and the Search for God in the Americas*, ed. María Clara Bingemer and Peter J. Casarella (Washington, DC: Catholic University of America Press, 2021), 224–49.

2. **Pastoral conversion** requires that leadership in the Church assume a practical, existential stance toward ministry, one that is more inductive than deductive. Ministries must become more accessible and less constrained by hierarchical and juridical concerns. The Church reveals itself as an instrument of God's all-inclusive tenderness and mercy rather than judgment and exclusion, a "field hospital in times of war."

3. Ecclesial leadership must be imbued with *servant qualities* and move away from an excessive and destructive concern for status. Jesus' remark in the Gospel of Mark to the effect that those who wish to be first must be the last of all and the servant of all (Mark 9:35) captures the underlying principle of ecclesial leadership. Closely related to this stance toward service rather than status is *synodality* which refers to the challenges of truly gaining as much as possible the *participation and engagement* of the whole people of God, thus putting to rest forever the old formulation about the laity's role in terms of "pray, pay, and obey." The servant and synodal approaches to leadership pay attention to where the Holy Spirit is leading the people of God. Hence, they reflect the co-essential nature of ecclesial ministry and individual charisms for building up the Church.[14]

4. By *leadership with a Hispanic/Latinx presence and flair* is meant a leadership that is integral to and for the particular charisms for Church and society of the Hispanic/Latinx cultures, a leadership that is congenial to the distinctive history, ways of thinking and feeling, and religious and spiritual sensibilities of the Hispanic/Latinx community. Such leadership will put a premium on cultural integration rather than assimilation or conformity

---

[14] Congregation for the Doctrine of the Faith, *Juvenescit Ecclesia* (Rome: May 15, 2016), 10.

to the middle class European American norm. It will reflect an ability to live with ambiguity by moving away from moralism and rigidity and toward an orientation to lively liturgical and social celebration. The Hispanic/Latinx presence will stress the integration of Church teaching with family and SCC activities, especially through *fiesta* and domestic religion. A Hispanic/Latinx ethos will foster a more robust, graphic religious aesthetic and an expanded repertoire of sacramentals.[15]

5. The Hispanic/Latinx presence in the United States serves to retrieve and renew the social justice legacy of US Catholicism that originated in the harsh socioeconomic reality of 19th and 20th century Catholic immigration. This legacy now takes on more urgency than ever in light of the crises of unauthorized immigration and growing inequality among 21st-century Hispanic/Latinx immigrants and other socially marginal groups. It calls for the promotion of *a Hispanic/Latinx leadership committed to reconciliation, justice, and peace*. Social justice challenges are not limited to migration issues but span an entire gamut of justice concerns, such as access to health care, housing, education, racism, and civil rights.[16] The CARA interviews reflect the concern of youth and young adult leaders for a broader focus on social-ethical concerns, a seamless garment approach to leadership that integrates faith, justice, and spirituality.

---

[15] Timothy Matovina, *Latino Catholicism: Transformation in America's Largest Church* (Princeton, NJ: Princeton University Press, 2012), 49. See also Timothy Matovina, "Latino Contributions to Vatican II Renewal: The Charles S. Casassa Lecture, Loyola Marymount University," *Origins* 42, no. 29 (December 2012): 465–71, and Allan Figueroa Deck, "Latino Migrations and the Transformation of Religion in the United States: Framing the Question," in *Christianities in Migration: The Global Perspective*, ed. Elaine Padilla and Peter C. Phan (New York: Palgrave Macmillan, 2016), 263–80.

[16] Matovina, *Latino Catholicism*, 190–218.

6. Finally, Hispanic/Latinx leadership, according to the
   Latino Pastoral Leadership Initiative, will find its *foun-
   dational sources* in the call of the Second Vatican Council
   and Pope Paul VI, especially in *Evangelii Nuntiandi*, for a
   dynamic conception of the Church understood as the
   people of God in history, a pilgrim people reaching out
   in service to all humanity. A new leadership will integrate
   Vatican II's Theology of the Church with Pope John Paul
   II's numerous contributions to the development of the
   Church's missionary dynamic, preferential option for the
   poor, and other features of Catholic Social Teaching. Pope
   Francis's landmark teachings in *Evangelii Gaudium, Lau-
   dato Si', Amoris Laetitia*, and *Fratelli Tutti* provide a rich
   and stimulating vision for servant leadership in times of
   epochal change.

These core elements of and for a new paradigm of Church
leadership grounded in Pope Francis's urgent call for pastoral
conversion offer constructive ways forward for meeting the
enormous challenge of the disaffiliation of young people from
the Church, as many of the findings of CARA's recent research
suggest. The work of the Leadership Roundtable and its Latino
Pastoral Leadership Initiative (LPLI) represents a promising
adaptation of that exciting vision of Church reform to the
emerging demographic and sociocultural realities of today's
US Catholicism moving forward.

CHAPTER SIX

The Experiences and Perspectives of Young Hispanics/Latines through the Pandemic

Claudia Avila Cosnahan

Pandemic Losses

When I met Jessica[1], she took an interest in my work. We were both millennials; she was in her mid-20s, and I was only a few years older than her. She asked about how I had become a lay ecclesial minister, my discernment, and my formation. We talked about our shared culture as Mexican Americans living in Southern California, faith, and spirituality. As a volunteer lay leader at the parish, she helped plan ministry and led Small Christian Community gatherings. I hoped I could offer her a safe place to lead, question, and dream. She felt a calling to serve the Church, and so I accompanied her throughout this period of her life. In the year prior to the pandemic, she was offered her first paid parish position. We had extensive conversations about the difficulties in ministry as women and as Latinas, but no amount of theoretical conversation could have spared her from the pain she endured there.

---

[1] This name has been changed for anonymity, and the story was shared with permission.

She said, "I was excited at the beginning. I thought this would be a real start to what I felt was my calling, but I soon realized that my ideas and my concerns were not taken seriously. I was the only person of color listening to the needs of the Latino community, and there were no resources available to them. I began to minister outside of my paid hours because I couldn't ignore them." She also shared, "When the pastor tried to start a young adult ministry, others on staff refused to take my advice, even though I was the only young adult on staff, and instead of choosing me to coordinate the ministry, the pastor asked a White deacon in his late 50s to coordinate."

Early in the COVID-19 pandemic, Jessica had ideas about how to be present to the community in a time when they could not gather at the parish, but she was met with anger from a pastor who didn't believe COVID-19 restrictions were necessary. Jessica said, "This was a time of opportunity for our parish to be a place of hope and a place that provided good information. We could have reached out. I wanted to do so much—I had the skills to do things online and with social media—but instead, my hours were cut so severely that I had to leave."

In this study, new membership in Small Christian Communities was a topic of concern to interviewees. Jessica, like many young lay ministers I've learned of anecdotally, have left their positions or were let go in the last two years. Interviewees in this study made "observations about insufficient number of people working with SCCs (i.e., paid staff and volunteer group leaders). A few stated that before the pandemic those human resources were very limited and that during the financial crises in parishes caused by the pandemic, SCCs' coordinators were among the first staff members to be laid off, which made the situation even more difficult."[2]

---

[2] Gray, Kramarek, and Gaunt, *Faith and Spiritual Life of Catholics*, 11.

Jessica said, "I left because I wasn't valued, I increasingly felt that racism had a hand in how I was being treated and how the community was neglected, and, ultimately, I realized that I could be of better service to others outside of the institutional Church. The institutional Church, in my eyes, failed to step in when we all needed its support the most."

I asked Jessica if she could imagine herself returning to paid parish ministry after the pandemic. She said she's healing and can't imagine herself doing that any time soon. She described the Church's response to the nation's reckoning with institutional racism and its failure in leading the faithful in the efforts to stop the spread of COVID-19 as her main disappointments. Additionally, she didn't want to work for an institution that didn't value her.

This study's poll revealed that 36 percent of the respondents expected to return to Mass with less frequency after stay-at-home orders are lifted and the pandemic has passed. Hispanic respondents, compared to non-Hispanic respondents, were even more likely to say they would not return, at 40 percent compared to 33 percent, respectively. However, when participants were asked about their faith, 71 percent of respondents said there had been no change in their Catholic faith—that is, there was no weakening or strengthening of their Catholic faith. Faith and institutional engagement may be conceived as two separate things.

The pandemic and the noteworthy events of the time seemingly accelerated the loss of young adult participation and engagement, particularly within ecclesial spaces where support was already lacking. It's important to consider the ramifications of lost lay ecclesial vocations, not only vocations to the priesthood or religious life. This time helped usher in what I would consider a crisis for the institutional Church, which will be greatly felt when older generations begin to retire in the not too distant future. If, prior to the pandemic, parishes were already lacking young leaders who can speak to their generation, who can take on serious positions of pastoral leadership, and who can naturally maneuver the landscape of modern communication, then we can anticipate that when the pandemic is, indeed, over, the crises of affiliation, Mass attendance, and leadership will be even greater.

Jessica has returned to in-person Mass, and only time and the Church's ability to listen and respond will tell what her engagement with the institutional Church will be like in the future. Consistent with the findings in this study, however, her faith continues to be important and a daily guiding force.

Prayer in Quarantine

Mass attendance cannot be the only criteria we use to measure religious engagement, especially when we consider the history and theology of spiritual and religious popular practices of Hispanic/Latine Catholics referenced earlier in this book by Allan Figueroa Deck, SJ. Prayer throughout the pandemic can serve as a locus for discerning the potential for leadership, especially when respondents to this study express great concern for the need for leaders who can guide Small Christian Communities. In the study, 28 percent of respondents increased their prayer practices throughout the pandemic, and females were more likely than males to say they prayed more since the pandemic began (32% compared to 24%).

On the first Sunday that the Archdiocese of Los Angeles closed all Masses to the public and went virtual, I felt a deep sorrow thinking that it was very likely that few to no women would receive communion in the parishes of my Archdiocese, myself included. Natalia Imperatori-Lee writes, "For marginalized communities like many Latino/a communities in the United States, who were frequently underserved by the Church with few Spanish-speaking clergy and little receptivity to their pastoral needs, popular Catholicism provided (and in many cases continues to provide) a lifeline to faith and spiritual sustenance. . . . Though they occur outside the parish, these practices are no less central to faith. Neither do they detract from major celebrations such as the Eucharist."[3]

The pandemic experience has been, for some individuals and communities, a time of being underserved by the Church. As a lay ecclesial minister, I had become so accustomed to being at the parish almost every day that when I began to work from home, I had to create a sacred space that would lend itself to spontaneous moments of prayer in a prominent location. I needed to create a prayerful environment for the Small Christian Communities I was leading virtually, and it needed to serve as an altar, close to our television so that it could accompany me and my husband as we celebrated Mass virtually. Our Lady of Guadalupe keeps prayer with me as she looks over my votive candle. I keep a statue of Divine Mercy because it connects me to my two deceased grandfathers, an open Bible in which I periodically change the open page according to my struggles and mood, a *copalero* to burn incense periodically, holy water and candles to aid me in my devotions, and many other things I've collected through my life that remind me of my relationship with God. Although there has been much about which to be depressed in the past two years, my popular religious practices have been a source of healing and empowerment.

Gente Puente (Bridge People)

This study revealed various instances in which Hispanics/ Latines are likely to find ways to flourish when the institutional Church cannot provide the support it needs. My concern is whether the present and future leadership of the Church can flourish without the guidance and perspective of young Hispanics/Latines. This is a generation of Catholics who are more

[3] Natalia Imperatori-Lee, *Cuéntame: Narrative in the Ecclesial Present* (Maryknoll, NY: Orbis Books, 2018), 24.

comfortable with questioning the institutional Church's engagement with LGBTQ+ issues, allegations of clergy sexual abuse, women's reproductive policies, the role of women in the Church, labor rights, and systemic racism, to name a few. Their comfortability with such issues is a gift to a Church and a nation in need of dialogue and synodality. First- and second-generation Hispanics/Latines are heirs to the popular religiosity that has sustained generations of marginalized Catholics. They are simultaneously privileged by their closeness to the fast-paced, constantly evolving digital landscape and deeply wounded by—and therefore passionate about—the socio, political, and economic crises of the last two decades.

Beyond Young Adult Ministry and Pastoral Hispana

Throughout the first year of the pandemic, I led three virtual Small Christian Communities, two of which had a membership that was majority Hispanic/Latine millennials. One of the groups was a Spanish language community that had been preparing for Confirmation. The group was made up of middle-aged immigrants from Central America and Mexico and young adults whose primary language was English but preferred a Spanish group because that was their faith language. The second group was an English language group made up entirely of millennials who had also been preparing for Confirmation prior to the pandemic. This group was relatively diverse, reflective of the demographics of Los Angeles, California, but with a majority Hispanic/Latine membership. We met weekly, and as we checked in on our well-being, we prayed together, reflected on scripture, and used the readings to reflect on the pandemic, racial issues, and the political turmoil of the time.

As many of the respondents shared in the study, these virtual gatherings were a source of hope and belonging in a time that was isolating. It's important to consider that, while the English language group included non-Hispanic members, it had aspects of pastoral Hispana because the Hispanic/Latine members of the group brought their culture and background with them into the space we created that allowed for each person to speak from their authentic experience. When I gathered with the Spanish-speaking group, the young adults clearly had experiences to share that were unique to them as US-born Hispanics/Latines, so they could have easily joined the English language group. Ministry to and with millennial Hispanics/Latines, particularly those who are the first generation born in the United States, does not fit easily into the categories that have been set for young adult ministry and pastoral Hispana. It is also the case that millennials in leadership are equipped to serve in other areas of ministry that go beyond young adult ministry.

As we move forward and take inventory of the losses suffered throughout the pandemic, it will be important to consider a new, dynamic approach to reaching out to millennial Hispanics/Latines who do not fit perfectly into the traditional models of young adult ministry empty of any cultural considerations. It will also be necessary to fill positions of leadership beyond young adult ministry with young Hispanic/Latine leaders so that this generation and the next ones are positioned to flourish within the institutional Church.

Listening and SCCs

The trends we see in the study, as highlighted in the earlier parts of this chapter, indicate that ministry to and with young Hispanics/Latines will require new methods and models of ministry that prioritize listening as a first step, with the primary objective of honoring the gifts of young people and providing a space where they can feel heard and understood. Concerns surrounding leadership, Mass attendance, and continued engagement with the institutional Church will require the Church to meet young Catholics where they are. Listening

to individual narratives will help local communities discover
their failings and their opportunities for growth.

Employing the work of Kenneth Davis, Natalia Imperatori-
Lee proposes that "SCCs could be formalized into the structure
of the Church if it were willing to designate personal parishes
chartered as a community of small communities."[4] Though
the model presents some challenges, one of the reasons she
argues that the SCC parish model is worth examining is because "demographic and sociological shifts in U.S. Catholics
call for a shift in tactics, a radical reimagining of how the
church functions in this society. As Davis notes, during 'the
last exodus of Catholics to Protestant churches [in the Refor-
mation], an ecumenical council was called [Trent], seminaries
were established, religious orders founded. The church was
willing to revisit any ecclesiastic structure that was no longer
addressing contemporary needs.'"[5]

Small Christian Communities can provide a space to grapple
with the pandemic experience. They can provide a space where
the Church can reconcile with those who have been disappointed by it, and they can encourage creativity to grow from
our experiences.

---

[4] Imperatori-Lee, *Cuéntame*, 115.
[5] Imperatori-Lee, 117. Imperatori-Lee quotes Davis, "Built from Living
Stones," 338.

CHAPTER SEVEN

Where Do We Go from Here?

Darius Villalobos

Where to Minister to Young Adults in the Post-Pandemic World

As we look ahead to the future of ministry in the post-pandemic era, there are lessons from the pandemic that need to be explored to help us understand where ministry should be happening next, especially with young adults. The question about where this should happen is important for a few reasons. First, Pope Francis has called the Church in *Christus Vivit* to make a renewed effort to meet young people "Where they are at."[1] This call should force pastoral agents to ask the question, "Where are young adults today?" This is not just a question of physical location, but it is also one that asks us to reflect and examine the content and context of our ministries.

Though many efforts have taken place over the years to reach young adults who have left the Church or never affiliated at all, we also have questions about the young adults who are engaged in parish life and whether they will return to in-person gatherings when our parishes are fully open. Some of their hesitations and frustrations with the Catholic Church stem from negative experiences in Church settings, taking issue with

---

[1] Pope Francis, Post-Synodal Apostolic Exhortation *Christus Vivit* (Rome: March 25, 2019).

some Church leaders and the rhetoric used to describe Church teachings in public, and the "authenticity gap" between what the Church teaches and preaches compared to the actions they see the Church taking. These questions about location challenge pastoral agents to look not only at the physical locations where we are trying to engage young adults, but also at the social locations the Church needs to occupy to be relevant in the lives of young people.

Online Gatherings

A reality learned from this study and the experiences had by young adults throughout the pandemic is the importance of online opportunities as a real place for young adult engagement. The ability to offer online spaces for community building was valuable for many young adult groups to keep connected and to continue their efforts while working through the pandemic. Though many young adult ministries took to Zoom and other virtual meeting apps to make continuing their ministry possible, the diversity of experiences in the virtual spaces was vast. From intimate small group discussions on articles and spiritual writings, to massive webinar events with speakers or panels, the kinds of virtual experiences were many. This past year, in the same week, I participated in an online retreat for young adults with forty participants broken into small groups of three to five people over the course of a week as well as a one-day program with young adults, ministry leaders, and clergy that had over four hundred live participants. Each experience was fruitful but vastly different. These efforts and their successes should challenge ministry leaders to continue virtual programming beyond the time of the pandemic. The diversity of people a ministry can reach and the accessibility it brings could allow virtual experiences to be entry points for new young adults to join a ministry, an important part of the evangelization process. It also allows young adults who are engaged but who cannot participate in these in-person minis-tries to stay engaged, including those who have moved out of the geographic area, those who have accessibility issues that do not allow them to attend, and those whose schedules would not allow them to participate in an in-person experi-ence. As stated in the report: "The opportunities identified in the interviews include the ease of access and the removal of geographic limitations on who can participate in the meetings (allowing for easier participation by, for example, people with disabilities, people who are sick, people without access to transportation, people living in different parts of the world, and people of different backgrounds)."[2] One pastoral question that I see arising is the question about geographic boundaries. Parishes are canonically defined by the geographic boundaries they are given. As the Code of Canon Law states, "As a general rule a parish is to be territorial, that is it embraces all the Chris-tian faithful within a certain territory; whenever it is judged useful, however, personal parishes are to be established based upon rite, language, the nationality of the Christian faithful within some territory or even upon some other determining factor."[3]

What are the boundaries of the digital territory? Can par-ishes continue to limit their ministry to the individuals that reside in their geographic boundaries? We already know that the practical realities of this canon rarely exist in many parishes today. Urban parishes are the best examples of this, where people will travel far distances to go back to the parish they grew up in, follow a pastor that they like, or visit the place that has the most convenient Mass time that fits into their sched-ules. Many young adults will travel to a parish that has a young adult ministry in which they find community and want

---

[2] Gray, Kramarek and Gaunt, *Faith and Spiritual Life of Catholics*, 12.

[3] *Code of Canon Law* (Washington, DC: Canon Law Society of America, 1983), c. 518.

to be close to their friends. When young adults move away from the neighborhood to another part of town, they often make efforts to go back and be with their friends, even if there is a parish that is in closer proximity to their new home. As we ask the question, "Where does the Church need to go to meet young adults?" we may also need to ask, "What are the limits of where a parish should go to reach young adults?" Parishes that quickly adopted virtual Mass experiences when the pandemic started and lockdown measures were adopted may see many new faces join them in person when Mass opportunities open in full. Parishes that were slow to adopt these virtual Mass experiences or never made the move could find that many of their young adults moved on to parishes that were better equipped to meet their need for prayer and community.

In recognizing the benefits of online opportunities, it is also important to recognize the limitations as well. It is harder to reach new young adults with these online programs. An interesting topic or speaker might catch the eye of a few young adults via social media, but the most effective way to get young adults to show up to a ministry gathering is through personal invitation. Personal invitation proves difficult if there is not an already established relationship that exists. An emphasis needs to be made to enable young adults to see themselves as the agents of evangelization efforts and to equip them with the tools needed to do this outreach. If personal invitations are the most successful way to grow young adult engagement, then parishes need to equip young adults with the tools needed to invite their peers to their ministries. This includes giving them the vocabulary to explain to others why this ministry is important, being transparent about the goals of this ministry, and making sure that the ministry is accessible for new members.

A good reflection question to measure a young adult ministry's ability to engage new participants is to ask current members: "Would you be comfortable inviting your friends to participate in this ministry with you? Why or why not?" Another helpful reflection question could be: "If you were to invite some to join this group, what would you tell them to encourage them to participate?" Helping young adults articulate answers to these questions can help ministries avoid the "club" mentality that can often creep into groups and avoid becoming exclusive or cliquish.

Spaces and Places

Though the most common location of meeting for groups was within a parish (41%), there were plenty of examples of other places where ministry with young adults takes place. Not surprising was schools, colleges, or universities (21%), but somewhat surprising was other public spaces not related to parish or Church life (21%). This shows that many young adults are not finding community in the traditional parish setting. Even if they are going to the parish for sacraments, most are gathering in community off the parish campus.

A troubling reality for parishes with young adults was the lack of outreach from parishes during the pandemic: "Overall, 18% of respondents say their parish has reached out to them during the pandemic. Among those in households registered with a parish, 34% indicate that their parish has reached out to them. This is less frequent among those in households that are not registered with a parish (7%)."[4] This low number shows a lack of outreach to and engagement of young adults by parishes.

Another challenging response was around the expectations young adults had for parish engagement moving forward: "In the post-pandemic future, 46% expect to participate with faith groups outside of their parish with the same frequency that they did prior to the pandemic. *Forty-one percent* expect to do

---

[4] Gray, Kramarek, and Gaunt, *Faith and Spiritual Life of Catholics*, 69.

this less frequently in the future compared to 13% who expect to do this more frequently."[5] This should be alarming to any minister. The idea that 41 percent of young adults are less likely to participate in faith groups at a time where rates of disaffiliation are so high cannot be encouraging to our evangelization efforts. We should not be surprised that, due to the lack of outreach from parishes to young adults and the lack of interest from young adults in engagement in groups outside of parishes, we will have many young adults no longer engaging with the Church post-pandemic.

This begs a question that we need to have stated before: "Where does ministry to young adults need to be taking place?" However, we must also ask: "What will the Catholic Church need to do to meet young adults 'where they are at' for our ministries to be effective?"

Investing Time in Personal Outreach by Young Adults

Peer ministry is an essential part of the next steps for our ministry with young adults. A transformation must occur in our ministries that centers young adults as the primary agents of ministry with other young adults, not the passive recipients of the Church's ministry. This requires an investment by Church ministers to work with the young adults we currently have engaged in different ways. Developing stronger personal relationships, forming them in their capacity to talk and share about their faith and why it is important to them, and mentoring them in the process of accompanying others will be essential to the Church's success in ministry with young adults. Ministries like FOCUS have proven successful in these models within the collegiate space. A starting point for parishes may be to renew the role of sponsors in the Rite of Christian Initiation for Adults (RCIA), specifically training some sponsors

[5] Gray, Kramarek, and Gaunt, 5.

Table 7.1

How much, if at all, have the following ever made you less likely to be active in parish life?

	Very	Somewhat	Only a little	Not at all
The Church's teachings on homosexuality	22%	20%	14%	44%
Allegations of Catholic clergy sexually abusing minors	21	23	17	40
The Church's teachings on the use of birth control	16	18	15	51
Feeling that older generations have too much influence in the parish	14	21	21	44
The roles available to women in the Church	14	18	17	51
My perception of the Church's participation in politics and elections	14	17	19	50
Feeling like the Church is not open to dialogue with other religious faiths	13	20	19	48
The Church's teachings on divorce and remarriage	13	19	18	51
Being asked for donations	11	18	24	47
The parish is not welcoming to different ethnic or cultural Catholic groups	10	15	15	60
The parish is not welcoming to a family member or friend	9	13	13	66
The parish is not very welcoming to young adults	7	18	17	58
Feeling like the parish is not sufficiently adhering to the traditions of the Church	7	15	14	65

Source: Data from *Faith and Spiritual Life of Catholics in the United States* (Washington, DC: Center for Applied Research in the Apostolate, 2021).

who could work closely with young adult candidates and catechumens.

Another key step will be providing resources that allow young adults to take the community experience outside of the parish campus. As more ministries happen offsite, parishes will need to be more intentional about sending young adults out with a clear understanding of what they can share with other young adults to bring them back in. This may require developing more digital resources hosted by the parish but that can be used in different settings. This level of autonomy for young adults must also be encouraged, seen as a natural part of young adult faith development, and supported by the parish. Young adults must feel like the parish leadership trusts them to go out and share the Good News.

Parishes may also want to look creatively at opportunities for partnership. Taking some ministries that have traditionally existed on the parish campus and convening them at a local café or restaurant might be a good way to bring attention about these groups to young adults who will never visit the parish. This may include speaker sessions (as in the original model of Theology on Tap), sports activities, and book and reading clubs, to name just a few examples. It may also require new activities to be developed that fit into a more secular setting, like trivia nights, mixers and networking events, or dances.

The Need for Relevancy

Finally, the content of these ministries needs to be relevant to the lives of young adults. The issues identified in the CARA study that have made young adults less likely to be active in parish life can be telling, as evidenced in Table 7.1.

The issues that young adults find troubling, which are likely keeping them at a distance from the Church, are areas that the Church often finds difficult to engage in conversation. Issues like the Church's teachings on sexuality, the role of women, and engaging in political life are usually framed as one-way conversations—the Church says this and you must believe it. Rarely do ministries address these issues in a conversational or dialogical way, where young adults can ask questions or share opinions and experiences. Other issues, like clergy sex abuse and tensions between older and younger Church members, do not get addressed at all in many Church spaces. The lack of conversation can be as damaging, if not more so, than a one-sided approach. And as difficult conversations around racism, diversity, and inclusion have increased in US society in recent years due to the deaths of African Americans by police, hate crimes against Asian Americans, and continued debates on the treatment of immigrants, the Church finds itself in self-reflection on moral issues that continue to be polarized in society by a political lens.

In the National Dialogue Final Report published in spring of 2021, it addressed the "authenticity gap" that exists between young people and the Church in the United States in this way: "Youth and young adults articulated negative attitudes and experiences that they describe as impatient judgement, polarizing division, and hypocrisy (and empty platitudes) within the Church on both the local and global levels. They also articulated the desire for authenticity of those who accompany them as they seek out a relationship with God and to discern their future."[6] This acknowledgment of the way young people experience the Church should challenge pastoral ministers to rethink their engagement on these issues that are relevant to the lives of young people. If we are not able or willing to engage in honest dialogue on these important issues with young adults, we should be ready for a continued distancing of young adults from our faith communities.

---

[6] *National Dialogue on Catholic Pastoral Ministry with Youth and Young Adults: Final Report* (Washington, DC: National Federation for Catholic Youth Ministry, 2021), 108.

Where Young Adult Ministry Should Take Place

The pandemic has given us a moment to pause and rethink our strategies for ministry with young adults. Parish communities, movements, campus ministry centers, and small faith sharing communities all have a moment to reimagine what their accompaniment of young adults can look like. A few lessons learned that we should consider:

• Continue to utilize online experiences even after we can gather in-person again. The accessibility for those that could not or cannot participate in in-person gatherings make these experiences even more valuable and allow for a diversity of programming that could help reach already engaged young adults as well as invite in new young adults to our ministries.

• An investment in young adults to be the protagonists in ministry to their peers is an important shift in our ministry models and a necessary one. If personal relationship and invitation is the most effective way to engage young adults in our ministries, we must equip young adults with the tools to do this outreach.

• A return to in-person gatherings should come with a renewed spark of creativity for parishes to move ministry beyond the parish campus. Finding local partners to expand where young adult outreach can take place can help ministry stay relevant and ensure that the Church is meeting young adults "where they are at."

• Church ministries need to engage young adults in conversations on relevant issues. This engagement cannot be simply passing along the Church's teachings on issues but must allow for honest dialogue, listening, and sharing of experiences so that young adults feel heard and accompanied by the Church in an authentic way.

Whatever the Church does beyond the current pandemic moment to engage young adults will be significant for the short-term and long-term future of the Catholic Church in the United States. If pastoral ministers approach their ministry as "business as usual," we may see the steady decline of young adult engagement and an increase in the growth of those disaffiliated from the Church. However, if we move our ministry with young adults to new spaces and places, we may find ourselves in authentic and exciting experiences with more young people who have a desire and need for what the Catholic Church has to offer.

CONCLUSION

Learnings

Thomas P. Gaunt, SJ

The CARA national survey of young adult Catholics in 2020 described in Chapter 1 challenges the common assumption that participation in the weekly Mass at a local parish is the measure for being actively engaged in one's Catholic faith. The national survey finds that about one in eight (13%) young adult Catholics attended Mass weekly or more often prior to the pandemic in 2020. On the other hand, six in ten (60%) young adult Catholics report regular participation in groups that practice their faith, provide service, or evangelize others. Weekly Mass attendance may not be a sufficiently robust measure of faith engagement for young adults.

When asked why they were not attending Mass weekly, more than half of young adult Catholics cited the demands of a busy schedule and their belief that missing Mass is not a sin as major reasons, while feeling alienated from the Church was cited by fewer than one in four. Young adults report that the Church's teaching on homosexuality, allegations of clergy sexual abuse, older generations having too much influence in the parish, and the roles available to women in the parish made them less likely to be active in their local parish. Local parish activities are not as available or attractive to young adults as they could be, with the result that many more young adult Catholics are actively engaging their faith life and commitments separate from and outside of their local parishes.

The CARA national survey of Small Christian Communities (SCC) and selected interviews with participants reviewed in Chapter 2 estimated that more than nine million or about 45 percent of young adult Catholics have regularly participated (at least once a quarter or seasonally) in an SCC as an adult. Hispanic, African American, Asian American, and those of other ethnicities are more likely than White Catholics to participate in SCCs. Through interviews, these cultural/ethnic differences were seen as a reflection of the individualistic ethos and agenda-driven focus of Whites in contrast to the more communal and relationship-driven focus of other ethnic and cultural groups.

The participants in SCCs generally (as compared to nonparticipants) had more engagement with parishes and more Catholic education growing up. They were also more likely to pray (individually and with others) and to be registered at a Catholic parish. They are motivated to participate in SCCs by a desire to learn from new experiences, nourish their spiritual life, reduce negative feelings, and develop and strengthen social ties with others.

Among the recommendations for future action, interviewees mention the need to recruit more paid staff and volunteer leaders to animate and initiate more SCCs. Local pastors and bishops need to offer encouragement and support for SCCs that may operate fairly separate from the parish. Church leaders need to actively listen to young adults on both an institutional and human level, giving them the space to engage their faith. This may often mean that different cultural/ethnic groups create different manners of engaging, expressing, and acting on their Catholic faith.

Chapter 3 focuses particular attention on those cultural/ethnic differences among SCCs and the implications for the future of Catholicism in the United States. Specifically, Hispanic SCCs are more likely to evangelize persons who want to grow in their faith, practice charismatic prayer, and go on retreats as well as to socialize together. These elements of an SCC may not be welcomed or encouraged in the dominant White anglophone parishes, thereby presenting an unwelcome face to Hispanic Catholics and others whose gifts to Catholicism in the United States may then be lost.

The great changes in family life and the evolution of our understanding of Catholic family life in the United States is described in Chapter 4. A Catholic understanding of family sees the family as the domestic church and family as a vocation. In recent decades, Catholic families are increasingly Hispanic Catholic families that expand culturally how faith is communicated from one generation to another. Because young adults are often at a distance from the local parish communities yet long for a sense of belonging, SCCs are often more accessible and engaging. SCCs may be the more effective means of communicating and sharing the richness and reality of the family as the domestic church, the family as vocation, to these young adults. Hispanic Catholics, drawing from rich cultural and religious traditions of profound communal character, bring a renewed passion for family life that often stands as countercultural to predominant individualistic social mores.

The domestic religious practices of Hispanic families and the emerging leadership of Hispanic Catholics in US Catholicism are examined in Chapter 5. The dominance of popular religious culture over ecclesiastical culture over time in Latin America is in contrast with the more "Anglo" experience in much of the US Church. The CARA research provides support for the idea that domestic and popular religion is alive and well, especially among Hispanic Catholics. The recent experience of the pandemic has strengthened the household religious experience as in-person engagement at the parish level was limited.

Popular Catholicism centered in the home can reconfigure ministry in the Church by emphasizing the agency of the family rather than the ordained. It is through baptism that one becomes a "missionary disciple." The experience of SCCs, particularly among Hispanic Catholics, is transforming leadership within the faith community that is more lay-centered, inclusive, and culturally competent.

This theme of popular Catholicism and the agency of young adult Hispanic leaders is further explored in Chapter 6. Faith and institutional engagement may be conceived as two separate things, particularly as the pandemic experience highlighted the importance and enduring value of popular religious practices. The larger Church needs to encourage young adult leadership, especially among groups in the Hispanic Catholic community. New models of ministry that prioritize listening as a first step are needed to provide a space of understanding among those who have been disappointed by the Church and to encourage creativity.

Chapter 7 looks at the question of where we meet young adults today as both a question of physical location and social location. The experience of the pandemic has changed the way we understand this question, with the increase in online opportunities as a real place for young adult engagement from the meeting of a few friends to massive webinar events. Traditionally, much pastoral activity occurred within geographic parish boundaries, but what are the new boundaries of digital faith engagement? The importance of personal invitation into being a part of a faith community is acknowledged, while asking how that personal invitation is extended in a digital realm. The CARA research documents the lack of outreach to young adults during the pandemic, a time when digital outreach and engagement was critical.

The importance of peer ministry—young adults as the primary agents of ministry with other young adults—is key to the Church's outreach. This ministry is likely to be outside of the parish campus at schools, cafés, and homes and must engage young adults with issues in the Church that they find troubling: sexuality, the role of women, and engaging in political life. It is the lack of conversation on these issues that distance young adults from the Church community. This is a challenge to pastoral ministers, who must be willing and able to engage in honest dialogue on these important issues with young adults.

APPENDIX

The CARA Research Studies Used in This Book

Michal J. Kramarek

This book is primarily based on a large-scale study conducted by the Center for Applied Research in the Apostolate with the purpose of exploring faith and spiritual life of Catholics in the United States (especially among young adults and Hispanics/Latinos) to help better understand their spiritual needs and how existing spiritual formation programs cater to these needs. More specifically, the study explored these questions: How do Catholics practice their faith in the United States? What role do Small Christian Communities play in the faith life of young adult Catholics in the United States? How can more young adult Catholics be attracted to join Small Christian Communities in the United States? What are the main challenges Small Christian Communities face?

To explore those questions, CARA's study was divided into three components: a national poll of young Catholics, a national survey of Small Christian Communities, and interviews with Catholics working with Small Christian Communities. The methodology employed for each of these components is described below.

National Poll of Young Catholics

CARA conducted a national poll with a final sample of 2,214 young adults between the ages of eighteen and thirty-five. The poll was administered between July and August 2020. The respondents were drawn from NORC's AmeriSpeak® Panel for the sample source (394 respondents). The AmeriSpeak sample was supplemented by nonprobability online opt-in sample (Dynata; 1,820 respondents). Due to the coronavirus pandemic occurring at the time of the survey, some of the study was dedicated to asking about faith practices and experiences with the Catholic community during the pandemic. This poll was offered in English and Spanish, and it was administered as an online web survey and telephone interview. The weighted AAPOR RR3 cumulative response rate for the poll was 4.2 percent. The margin of sampling error for the sample is ±3.59 percent.

When the survey was in the field, the Census estimated the US population to be 328,239,523. Of this population, 97,732,596 are young adults between the ages of eighteen and thirty-five. The 2018 General Social Survey (GSS) estimates that 21.1 percent of this demographic self-identifies as Catholic. Thus, the universe from which our sample is drawn includes 20,621,578 young adult Catholics between the ages of eighteen and thirty-five. Every 1 percentage point in the overall sample can be extrapolated as representing approximately 206,000 individuals in the population.

National Survey of Small Christian Communities

CARA conducted a national survey of Small Christian Communities, which for the purpose of this study were defined as groups that have at least some Catholic members, are located in the United States, and are not communities of men or women religious. Despite being called Small Christian Communities, some of the groups may have a large number of members. It was up to the study participants to define what small means. Some groups may have a large number of members but still are able to offer small community experiences. The survey was in the field in Spanish and English, using an online instrument, between November 2019 and July 2020. The survey was disseminated using snowball sampling. Initially, CARA identified forty-seven national associations of Small Christian Communities. CARA asked them to electronically forward a survey invitation to their members. Each of those associations was contacted at least three times. As a result, fifteen associations opted out of participation in the study, nineteen did not respond, and thirteen agreed to participate in the study. Additionally, CARA contacted 177 Hispanic ministry diocesan offices and 14,361 Catholic parishes inviting them to forward the survey invitation to their small groups. Survey participants were encouraged to invite others to participate. The final sample included 646 groups.

Interviews about Small Christian Communities

CARA selected interviewees from a list of 192 respondents to the National Survey of Small Christian Communities who opted in to participate in the interviews, a list of seventeen contacts from national associations of Small Christian Communities, and a list of eight other professionals working in the field. CARA selected contacts for interviews prioritizing Hispanics, young adults, and individuals with broad (national or international) perspective and long-term experience.

The interviews were conducted in English and Spanish between July and September, 2020, by means of video calls (using Zoom) and phone calls. Overall, twenty-two interviews were completed: fourteen with English-speaking Catholics and eight with Spanish-speaking Catholics working with Small Christian Communities in the United States. The interviewees included pastors, university professors/researchers, and parish and diocesan staff members, as well as leaders of national and international umbrella organizations fostering Small Christian Communities in the Catholic Church—in particular, youth groups, campus groups, young adult groups, and Hispanic/ Latino groups. All the interviews were recorded, with the explicit permission of the participants. Interviews in English were transcribed, while interviews in Spanish were summarized in detailed notes.

References

Baylor Institute for Studies of Religion. "Current Research." *Religion Watch* 29, no. 6 (2014).

Bengtson, Vern L., R. David Hayward, Merril Silverstein, and Philip Zuckerman. "Bringing Up Nones: Intergenerational Influences and Cohort Trends." *Journal for the Scientific Study of Religion* 57, no. 2 (2018): 258–76.

Bianchi, Enrique Ciro. *Pobres en este mundo, ricos en la fe.* Buenos Aires: Libros Agape, 2012.

Blackstone, Amy. " 'It's just about being fair': Activism and the Politics of Volunteering in the Breast Cancer Movement." *Gender & Society* 18, no. 3 (2004): 350–68.

Bruge, Guy. "Behind the Steep Decline in Church Attendance among Women." *State of the Church* (blog). *Barna Group*, March 4, 2020. https://www.barna.com/?s=Behind+the+steep+decline+in+church+attendance+among+women.

Bullivant, Stephen. *Mass Exodus: Catholic Disaffiliation in Britain and America since Vatican II.* New York: Oxford University Press, 2019.

Bumpass, Larry L. and James A. Sweet. "National Estimates of Cohabitation." *Demography* 26, no. 4 (November 1989): 619.

Callahan, Edward R. "Divorce: A Survey." *The American Catholic Sociological Review* 9, no. 3 (October 1948): 164.

Carroll, Colleen. *The New Faithful: Why Young Adults Are Embracing Orthodoxy.* Chicago: Loyola University Press, 2004.

Center for Applied Research in the Apostolate. "Declining Proportion of Baptisms a Cause for Concern." *The CARA Report* 19, no. 1 (2013): 3.

Chan, Melissa, Kim M. Tsai, and Andrew Fuligni. "Changes in Religiosity across the Transition to Young Adulthood." *Journal of Youth and Adolescence* 44, no. 8 (2015): 1555–66.

Clary, E. Gil, Mark Snyder, Robert D. Ridge, John Copeland, Arthur A. Stukas, Julie Haugen, and Peter Miene. "Understanding and Assessing the Motivations of Volunteers: A Functional Approach." *Journal of Personality and Social Psychology* 74, no. 6 (1998): 1516–30.

Clydesdale, Tim, and Kathleen Garces-Foley. *The Twenty-Something Soul: Understanding the Religious and Secular Lives of American Young Adults.* New York: Oxford University Press, 2019.

Code of Canon Law. Washington, DC: Canon Law Society of America, 1983.

Congregation for the Doctrine of the Faith. Letter *Juvenescit Ecclesia.* Rome: May 15, 2016.

Cugno, Franco, and Mario Ferrero. "Competition among Volunteers." *European Journal of Political Economy* 20, no. 3 (2004): 637–54.

D'Antonio, William V. "Communitas Celebrating Twenty Years of Building Community." In Healey and Hinton, *Small Christian Communities Today: Capturing the New Moment,* 49–54.

D'Antonio, William V., James D. Davidson, Dean R. Hoge, and Katherine Meyer. *American Catholics: Gender, Generation, and Commitment.* Lanham, MD: Rowman and Littlefield, 2001.

D'Antonio, William V., James D. Davidson, Dean R. Hoge, and Mary L. Gautier. *American Catholics Today: New Realities of Their Faith and Their Church.* Lanham, MD: Rowman and Littlefield, 2007.

D'Antonio, William V., Michele Dillon, and Mary L. Gautier. *American Catholics in Transition.* Lanham, MD: Rowman and Littlefield, 2013.

Davidson, James D., Andrea S. Williams, Richard A. Lamanna, Jan Steftenagel, Kathleen Maas Weigert, William J. Whalen, and Patricia Wittberg. *The Search for Common Ground: What Unites and Divides Catholic Americans.* Huntington, IN: Our Sunday Visitor Press, 1997.

Davis, Kenneth G. "Built from Living Stones: Hispanic Catholic Parishes Without Boundaries or Buildings." *New Blackfriars* 88, no. 1015 (2007): 335–52.

Dean, Kendra Creasy. *Almost Christian: What the Faith of Our Teenagers Is Telling the American Church.* New York: Oxford University Press, 2010.

Deck, Allan Figueroa. "Clericalism: Neuralgic Point of Church Reform." In *Pope Francis and the Search for God in the Americas,* edited by María Clara Bingemer and Peter J. Casarella, 224–49. Washington, DC: Catholic University of America Press, 2021.

Deck, Allan Figueroa. *Francis, Bishop of Rome: the Gospel for the Third Millennium.* New York: Paulist Press, 2016.

Deck, Allan Figueroa. "Latino Migrations and the Transformation of Religion in the United States: Framing the Question." In *Christianities in Migration: The Global Perspective,* edited by Elaine Padilla and Peter C. Phan, 263–80. New York: Palgrave Macmillan, 2016.

DeGuide, Susan, and Steven Valenzuela. "Development of SFCs in the Diocese of San Bernardio, California." In Healey and Hinton, *Small Christian Communities Today: Capturing the New Moment,* 41–48.

Denton, Melinda Lundquist, and Richard Flory. *Back-Pocket God: Religion and Spirituality in the Lives of Emerging Adults.* New York: Oxford University Press, 2020.

DeRogatis, Emily. *Saving Sex: Sexuality and Salvation in American Evangelicalism.* New York: Oxford University Press, 2015.

Dugan, Katherine. *Millennial Missionaries: How a Group of Young Catholics Is Trying to Make Catholicism Cool.* New York: Oxford University Press, 2019.

Espín, Orlando O. "Popular Catholicism." In *An Introductory Dictionary of Theology and Religious Studies,* edited by Orlando O. Espín and James B. Nickoloff, 1058–59. Collegeville, MN: Liturgical Press, 2007.

Espín, Orlando O. "Popular Religions." In *An Introductory Dictionary of Theology and Religious Studies,* edited by Orlando O. Espín and James B. Nickoloff, 1059–60. Collegeville, MN: Liturgical Press, 2007.

Faggioli, Massimo. *Sorting Out Catholicism: A Brief History of the New Ecclesial Movements.* Collegeville, MN: Liturgical Press, 2014.

Farrell, Justin. "The Young and the Restless? The Liberation of Young Evangelicals." *Journal for the Scientific Study of Religion* 50, no. 3 (2011): 517–32.

Fifth General Conference of the Latin American and Caribbean Bishops. *Aparecida Document*. Aparecida, Brazil: 2007.

Fry, Richard. "For First Time in Modern Era, Living with Parents Edges Out Other Living Arrangements for 18- to 34-Year-Olds." *Pew Research Center*, May 24, 2016.

General Social Survey. Chicago: National Opinion Research Center (NORC), 2000.

General Social Survey. Chicago: National Opinion Research Center (NORC), 2018.

Gray, Mark M. "A Dip in the Adult Catholic Population." *Nineteen Sixty-four* (blog). *Center for Applied Research in the Apostolate*, March 12, 2018. http://nineteensixty-four.blogspot.com/2018/03/a-dip-in-adult-catholic-population.html.

Gray, Mark M. "Exclusive Analysis: National Catholic Marriage Rate Plummets." *Our Sunday Visitor*, June 26, 2011. http://www.osv.com/tabid/7621/itemid/8053/Exclusive-analysis-National-Catholic-marriage-rat.aspx (site discontinued).

Gray, Mark M. *The U.S. Catholic Family: Demographics. The Second Special Report*. Washington, DC: Center for Applied Research in the Apostolate, 2015.

Gray, Mark M., Michal J. Kramarek, and Thomas P. Gaunt. *Faith and Spiritual Life of Catholics in the United States*. Washington, DC: Center for Applied Research in the Apostolate, 2021.

Gray, Mark M., Paul M. Perl, and Tricia C. Bruce. *Marriage in the Catholic Church: A Survey of U.S. Catholics*. Washington, DC: Center for Applied Research in the Apostolate, 2007.

Hardy, Phillip R., Kelly L. Kandra, and Brian G. Patterson. *Joy and Grievance in an American Diocese*. Lisle, IL: Benedictine University, 2014.

Healey, Joseph G., and Jeanne Hinton, eds. *Small Christian Communities Today: Capturing the New Moment*. Maryknoll, NY: Orbis Books, 2005.

Hegy, Pierre. *Wake Up, Lazarus!: On Catholic Renewal*. Self-published: iUniverse, 2012.

Hoffman, John P. "Declining Religious Authority? Confidence in the Leaders of Religious Organizations, 1973–2010." *Review of Religious Research* 55, no. 1 (2013): 1–25.

Hout, Michael, and Claude S. Fischer. "Explaining Why More Americans Have No Religious Preference: Political Backlash and Generational Succession, 1987–2012." *Sociological Science* 1 (2014): 423–46.

Howard, Thomas Albert. "Enough Bromides." *Commonweal* 148, no. 5 (May 2021): 34–37.

Howard, Thomas Albert. *The Faith of Others: A History of Interreligious Dialogue*. New Haven, CT: Yale University Press, 2021.

Imperatori-Lee, Natalia. *Cuéntame: Narrative in the Ecclesial Present*. Maryknoll, NY: Orbis Books, 2018.

Jacobs, Douglas, Douglas Tilstra, Finbar Benjamin, Sharon Pittma, Hollis James, Jerome Thayer, Thandi Klingbiel, Jordan Arellano, and Chelsy Tyler. "Adventist Millennials: Measuring Emerging Adults' Connection to Church." *Review of Religious Research* 61, no. 1 (2019): 39–56.

Jenner, Jessica R. "Participation, Leadership, and the Role of Volunteerism among Selected Women Volunteers." *Journal of Voluntary Action Research* 11, no. 4 (1982): 27–38.

Jones, Robert, Betsy Cooper, Daniel Cox, and Rachel Lienesch. *Exodus: Why Americans Are Leaving Religion—and Why They're Unlikely to Come Back*. Washington, DC: Public Religion Research Institute, 2016.

Kim, Stephen. *Memory and Honor: Cultural and Generational Ministry with Korean American Communities*. Collegeville, MN: Liturgical Press, 2010.

Koenig, Harold G., and Arndt Büssing. "The Duke University Religion Index (DUREL): A Five-Item Measure for Use in Epidemiological Studies." *Religions* 1, no. 1 (2010): 78–85.

Konieczny, Mary Ellen. *The Spirit's Tether: Family, Work, and Religion among American Catholics*. New York: Oxford University Press, 2013.

Lee, Bernard. *The Catholic Experience of Small Christian Communities*. New York: Paulist Press, 2000.

Lee, Bernard, and Michael Cowan. "Priority Concerns of SCCs in American Catholicism." In Healey and Hinton, *Small Christian Communities Today: Capturing the New Moment*, 63–72.

Madden, Nate. "Despite Low Catholic Marriage Numbers, Some See Trend Turning Around." *National Catholic Reporter*, March 23, 2015. https://www.ncronline.org/news/parish/despite-low -catholic-marriage-numbers-some-see-trend-turning-around/.

Manning, Wendy D., Susan L. Brown, and Krista K. Payne. "Does Cohabitation Compensate for Marriage Decline?" *Contexts* 20, no. 2 (May 2021): 68–69.

Matovina, Timothy. *Latino Catholicism: Transformation in America's Largest Church*. Princeton, NJ: Princeton University Press, 2012.

Matovina, Timothy. "Latino Contributions to Vatican II Renewal: The Charles S. Casassa Lecture, Loyola Marymount University." *Origins* 42, no. 29 (December 2012): 465–71.

McCarty, Robert J., and John M. Vitek. *Going, Going, Gone: The Dynamics of Disaffiliation in Young Catholics*. Winona, MN: St. Mary's Press, 2017.

McClure, Paul K. "Faith and Facebook in a Pluralistic Age: The Effects of Social Networking Sites on the Religious Beliefs of Emerging Adults." *Sociological Perspectives* 59, no. 4 (2016): 818–34.

Mintie, Dan. "Why Divorced Catholics Won't Just Go Away." *U.S. Catholic* 49, no. 10 (October 1984): 6–12.

Musick, Mark A., and John Wilson. "Volunteering and Depression: The Role of Psychological and Social Resources in Different Age Groups." *Social Science & Medicine* 56, no. 2 (2003): 259–69.

Musick, Mark A., and John Wilson. *Volunteers: A Social Profile*. Bloomington, IN: Indiana University Press, 2007.

Nanko-Fernández, Carmen. "Lo Cotidiano as Locus Theologicus." In *The Wiley Blackwell Companion to Latino/a Theology*, edited by Orlando O. Espín, 15–34. Chichester, West Sussex: Wiley Blackwell, 2015.

National Federation for Catholic Youth Ministry. *National Dialogue on Catholic Pastoral Ministry with Youth and Young Adults: Final Report*. Washington, DC: National Federation for Catholic Youth Ministry, 2021.

Newport, Frank. "An Update on Catholics in the U.S." *Gallup*, August 21, 2018. https://news.gallup.com/opinion/polling-matters/241235/update-catholics.aspx.

Newport, Frank. "U.S. Catholic Population: Less Religious, Shrinking." *Gallup*, February 25, 2013. http://www.gallup.com/poll/160691 (site discontinued).

Ospino, Hosffman. "Hispanics and Family Life in Twenty-First Century America: A Catholic Call to Action." In *Renewing Catholic Family Life and Spirituality: Experts Explore New Directions in Family Spirituality and Family Ministry*, edited by Gregory K. Popcak, 299–312. Huntington, IN: Our Sunday Visitor, 2020.

Perry, Samuel L., and Kyle C. Longest. "Examining the Impact of Religious Initiation Rites on Religiosity and Disaffiliation over Time." *Journal for the Scientific Study of Religion* 58, no. 4 (2019): 891–904.

Pew Forum on Religion and Public Life. *'Nones' on the Rise: One-In-Five Adults Have No Religious Affiliation*. Washington, DC: Pew Research Center, 2012.

Pope Francis. Apostolic Exhortation *Evangelii Gaudium*. Rome: November 24, 2013.

Pope Francis. Post-Synodal Apostolic Exhortation *Amoris Laetitia*. Rome: March 19, 2016.

Pope Francis. Post-Synodal Apostolic Exhortation *Christus Vivit*. Rome: March 25, 2019.

Pope John Paul II. Apostolic Exhortation *Familiaris Consortio*. Rome: November 22, 1981.

Pope John Paul II. Encyclical *Redemptoris Missio: On the Permanent Validity of the Church's Missionary Mandate*. Rome: December 7, 1990.

Pope Paul VI. Apostolic Exhortation *Evangelii Nuntiandi*. Rome: December 8, 1975.

Porteous, Julian. *A New Wine and Fresh Skins: Ecclesial Movements in the Church*. Cleveland, Australia: Modotti Press, 2010.

Public Religion Research Institute. *Dueling Realities: Amid Multiple Crises, Trump and Biden Supporters See Different Realities and Futures for the Nation*. Washington, DC: Public Religion Research Institute, 2020.

Puffer, Keith A. "Protestant Millennials, Religious Doubt, and the Local Church." *Religions* 9, no. 8 (2017).

Putnam, Robert D., and David E. Campbell to Allan Figueroa Deck, SJ. "The Changing Face of American Catholicism: A Memo." Washington, DC, May 22, 2008.

Reynolds, Philip Lyndon. *How Marriage Became One of the Sacraments: The Sacramental Theology of Marriage from Its Medieval Origins to the Council of Trent.* New York: Cambridge University Press, 2016.

Sadowski, Dennis. "Poll Finds Church Membership Continues Downward Trend in the 21st Century." *Catholic News Service*, March 31, 2021. https://www.catholicsun.org/2021/03/31/poll-finds -church-membership-continues-downward-trend-in-21st -century/.

Schuldt, Richard, Barbara Ferrara, and Ed Wojcicki. *Profile of Illinois: An Engaged State. Illinois Civic Engagement Benchmark Survey Results.* Springfield, IL: Illinois Civic Engagement Project, 2001.

Sciupac, Elizabeth Podrebarac. "Hispanic Teens Enjoy Religious Activities with Parents, but Fewer View Religion as 'Very Important.'" *Pew Research Center*, September 22, 2020. https://www .pewresearch.org/fact-tank/2020/09/22/hispanic-teens-enjoy -religious-activities-with-parents-but-fewer-view-religion-as -very-important/.

Second Vatican Council. Dogmatic Constitution on the Church, *Lumen Gentium*, November 21, 1964.

Second Vatican Council. Pastoral Constitution on the Church in the Modern World, *Gaudium et Spes*, December 7, 1965.

Segal, Lewis M., and Burton A. Weisbrod. "Volunteer Labor Sorting Across Industries." *Journal of Policy Analysis and Management* 21 (2002): 427–47.

Smietana, Bob. "Why No One May Be Getting Married at Your Church This Summer." *Facts and Trends*, May 31, 2018. https://research .lifeway.com/2018/05/31/why-no-one-may-be-getting -married-at-your-church-this-summer/.

Smith, Christian, Kyle Longest, Jonathan Hill, and Kari Christoffersen. *Young Catholic America: Emerging Adults In, Out of, and Gone from the Church.* New York: Oxford University Press, 2014.

Smith, Christian, and Patricia Snell. *Souls in Transition: The Religious and Spiritual Lives of Emerging Adults*. New York: Oxford University Press, 2009.

Smith, Tom W., Michael Davern, Jeremy Freese, and Stephen Morgan. *General Social Surveys, 1972–2018*. Chicago: National Opinion Research Center (NORC), 2019.

Sokolowski, S. Wojciech. "Show Me the Way to the Next Worthy Deed: Towards a Microstructural Theory of Volunteering and Giving." *Voluntas* 7 (1996): 259–78.

Thiessen, Joel, and Sarah Wilkins-LaFlamme. "Becoming a Religious None: Irreligious Socialization and Disaffiliation." *Journal for the Scientific Study of Religion* 56, no. 1 (2017): 64–82.

Thiessen, Joel, and Sarah Wilkins-LaFlamme. *None of the Above: Non-Religious Identity in the U.S. and Canada*. New York: New York University Press, 2020.

Third General Conference of Latin America and Caribbean Bishops. *Puebla Document*. Puebla, Mexico: 1979.

Toppe, Christopher M., Arthur D. Kirsch, and Jocabel Michel. *Giving and Volunteering in the United States: Findings from a National Survey, 2001 Edition*. Washington, DC: Independent Sector, 2001.

Twenge, Jean M. *iGen: Why Today's Super-Connected Kids Are Growing Up Less Rebellious, More Tolerant, Less Happy—And Completely Unprepared for Adulthood*. New York: Atria Books, 2017.

Twenge, Jean M., Julie J. Exline, Joshua B. Grubbs, Ramya Sastry, and W. Keith Campbell. "Generational and Time Period Differences in American Adolescents' Religious Orientation, 1966–2014." *Public Library of Science ONE* 10, no. 5 (2015): e0121454.

Vandenakker, John Paul. *Small Christian Communities and the Parish: An Ecclesiological Analysis of the North American Experience*. Kansas City, MO: Sheed & Ward, 1994.

Woodhead, Linda. "The Rise of 'No Religion': Towards an Explanation." *Sociology of Religion* 78, no. 3 (2017): 247–62.

Index